10 QUALITIES
OF THE WORLD'S
GREATEST
COMMUNICATORS

10 QUALITIES OF THE WORLD'S GREATEST COMMUNICATORS

Tony Alessandra

MEDIA

Published 2019 by Gildan Media LLC
aka G&D Media
www.GanddDmedia.com

FIRST EDITION 2019

Front Cover design by David Rheinhardt of Pyrographx

Interior design by Meghan Day Healey of Story Horse, LLC

Library of Congress Cataloging-in-Publication Data is available upon request

ISBN: 978-1-7225-0026-9

10   9   8   7   6   5   4   3   2   1

Contents

Introduction   1

Overview of the 10 Qualities   5

The Art of Asking Questions   21

The Power of Listening   35

Feedback   51

Concentration and Focus   67

Strengthening and Improving
Your Memory   81

Conflict Resolution   93

Presentation Power   109

Communication Adaptability   125

How to Use Space and Time to
Your Communication Advantage   141

Energy and Aura   155

Summary: Putting It All Together   169

Introduction

Almost every problem, every conflict, every mistake and every misunderstanding has a communication problem at its most basic level. As philosopher and psychologist William James observed, "The most immutable barrier in nature is between one man's thoughts and another's." I believe that while communication problems may never be completely eliminated, they can be reduced and often avoided.

We live in a world filled with other people where we live together, work together, and play together. In our personal lives, we need each other for security, comfort, friendship, and love. And in our working environment, we need each other in order to achieve our goals and objectives. None of these goals can be achieved without communication, which makes it the basic thread that ties us together. Through communication, we make known our needs, our wants, our ideas, and our feelings.

The better we are at communicating, the more effective we are at achieving our hopes and dreams.

I think it's fair to say that the majority of the great leaders in the worlds of both politics and business are also great communicators. They have an ability to establish bonds with people that are based on respect and honest communication. Great communicators make others want to trust and believe in them, and they possess a set of skills that enable them be heard in a way that gets results.

But wait, you might be thinking "I'll never be as good at communicating as history's great leaders. They had natural abilities that made them great!" And of course, to some extent, that's true. But it's also true that many of the qualities of the world's greatest communicators are finely honed skills that you too can develop with study and practice. We'll focus on ten of these qualities in this book. In just a moment, I'll give you a brief overview of the ten, but first, let me tell you how I was asked by the publisher to write this book and how I arrived at the qualities that I chose.

I started teaching human relations and other business courses at Susquehanna University in September 1970 and taught sales and marketing courses, with a heavy emphasis on communications, at various universities through the end of 1978. I remember telling one of my close friends that one day I wanted to rise to become a university president. He told me that wouldn't happen because my strong Brooklyn accent (deese, dem, dose & youse guys) would be my downfall during interviews. That hurt my feelings but I took it as a challenge to improve my accent and communication skills. In fact, in early 1979, I became, and still am a full-time professional speaker focusing on sales, relationship strategies and interpersonal communications. This was an occupation where I personally had to double my efforts to hone my communication skills, because my strong New York/ Brooklyn accent might have not made me sound as smart as someone with a PhD. I worked hard on my accent and communication skills, observing and studying the world's finest speakers, and improved to the point where I was eventually inducted into the **National Speakers Association "Speakers Hall of Fame"** in 1985. In fact, in 2012, I was voted the **#1 World's Top Communication Guru.**

Over the years, I have written 30 books, all with at least one section on effective communications including a book solely on communication skills titled *Communicating at Work*, with 18 chapters on different communication skills.

If you are thinking there must be more than just ten qualities, you would be right. So one of the most challenging aspects of writing this was to determine which are the top ten. I relied on three things to narrow it down. First, I drew on my 45 years of experience in teaching, researching, writing and speaking. This includes my years of teaching communications, specifically how it impacts relationship skills. Next, in preparing this specific material, I conducted research on the internet to gain insights from other great thinkers regarding the important qualities of communicators. And thirdly, I reached out through social media to my vast network of contacts to get their feedback on the subject. Combining these three areas of input, I created my list of the **Ten Qualities of Great Communicators** that are covered in this book. Following is a brief summary of each one.

Overview of the 10 Qualities

First, great communicators have mastered the art of asking questions. Questions can build rapport and trust, or foster suspicion and dislike. They can open up a conversation or shut it down. They can generate information or send a conversation off on a tangent. Questions can be used for many reasons in addition to the basic information gathering classics of Who, What, Where, When, Why and How. They are also used to stimulate a conversation, to determine another's views, to check agreement, to build rapport and trust, and to verify information. This chapter will help you understand how to use questions to improve your communication, what types of questions to use and when to use them, and the strategies and techniques of artful questioning. Being able to ask the right question at the right time is a crucial piece of the communication process.

The second quality is that great communicators are great listeners. Ineffective listening is one of the most frequent causes of misunderstandings, mistakes and problems. It's acknowledged to be one of the primary contributors to divorce and issues between parents and children. People view poor listeners as boorish, self-centered, preoccupied or disinterested—all barriers to effective communication. On the other hand, active listening is as powerful as speech, which is why great communicators are also active listeners. They're able to focus their attention on the thoughts and feelings of others as well as their own spoken word. They refrain from coming to premature judgments, and instead work to understand others' points of view. In this chapter, I'll discuss the six separate skills that great communicators develop to a high level of proficiency. They are combined into an easy-to-remember model with the acronym CARESS, which stands for concentrate, acknowledge, research, exercise emotional control, sense the nonverbal message and structure. Mastering these skills will be a powerful step toward becoming a great communicator, for let's always remember that what others say to you is just as critical as what you have to say to them.

Third, great communicators are highly skilled at giving and receiving feedback. Whenever you verbally, vocally or visually react to what another person says or does, or whenever you seek a reaction from another person to what you say or do, you are using feedback. Effective two-way communication depends on it. Good feedback, both verbal and nonverbal, can reduce interpersonal tension, while clarifying messages and uncovering important needs or problems. Through feedback, you can determine where to put your emphasis or where to spend less time. It's important to confirm all unclear verbal, vocal and observable cues through feedback. Its proper and effective use leads to an increased sense of mutual understanding, trust, and credibility. This chapter will explore the three key forms of feedback—verbal feedback, nonverbal feedback and feeling feedback--as well as how to use each form most effectively. Each serves a specific purpose in the communications process.

Fourth, great communicators have the ability to harness their powers of concentration and focus in order to send and receive their messages effectively. I know we've all experienced the barriers to effective communication—both external and internal. External barriers are mostly environmental—competing noises in a crowded restaurant, for example. Other external barriers have to do with the speaker—an odd accent, mannerism, or the pace of delivery, for example. Additional barriers result from the content of what's being said, such as using too many 'buzzwords.' Internal barriers that may come from you can be a challenge to overcome. These can be physical—you're sleep deprived, or physiological—you're daydreaming, perhaps. In this chapter, I'll give you some tips for handling these kinds of issues that are concentration and focus barriers and thus barriers to effective communication.

Fifth, great communicators have strong memories. Memory has traditionally been considered an aspect of intelligence, like a 'memory gene' perhaps. The fact is that memory is a skill you can develop and improve, just as you can get better at running or swimming. Just the simple concept of remembering someone's name can be a powerful connection to someone you're speaking with. But making the most of your memory power is not something that happens by itself. The process of memory has three parts: encoding, which is the formation of memory; memory storage; and finally, recall of stored memories. In this chapter, I'll talk more about what happens in the memory process. Then, you'll learn some specific techniques for developing and improving your short-term and long-term memory for maximum effectiveness.

Sixth, great communicators know how to engage in conflict resolution effectively. Conflict arises from the clash of perceptions, goals, or values in an arena where people care about the outcome. People naturally disagree about what to do and how and when to do it. When done skillfully, that interaction of ideas and opinions creates new ideas and leads to better solutions and action plans. This chapter will help you identify the sources of conflict and understand how to encourage healthy disagreement without spiraling down into a negative conflict. I will also talk about tools that will help you break out of a conflict routine once it has begun.

Seventh, great communicators are great presenters. This may seem obvious, but in reality, it has been found that the ability to make public presentations is the number one predictor of the level of professional success. And yet, it's the number one fear of most adults. So if you can master this skill, you have huge leg up on the ladder of being a world-class communicator. One way to approach this concept is to consider that almost all of our speaking (outside the shower anyway) is public speaking, it's just the size of the audience that changes. Good presentations provide opportunities for growth in power, recognition and prestige. Effective public speakers establish themselves as experts to whom others can turn to for advice. This chapter covers some simple guidelines that help you build good presentation skills. I'll cover such topics as overcoming stage fright, preparation for a successful presentation, and using audio-visual aids effectively.

Eighth, great communicators are able to practice communication adaptability in any given situation in a way that builds relationships. This quality involves two key skills—flexibility, which is one's willingness to adapt; and versatility, which is one's ability to adapt. Developing high adaptability allows you to speak many different 'behavior style languages' and understand how different types of people prefer to be treated. It involves making strategic adjustments to your methods of communicating and behaving. Adaptable people make the choice to go beyond their own comfort zone so that others feel more comfortable with them.

The ninth quality is knowing how to use space and time to one's maximum advantage. We are territorial creatures, and I think it's safe to say we are affected every day by how we and others use these two powerful communication tools. For example, if you violate someone's physical comfort zone (in other words, their personal space) by standing or sitting too close to them or touching them when they think you shouldn't, you may offend them and cause tension. Similarly, If you abuse another's sense of time—by being too early or too late, or by leaving too quickly or staying too long—well, you get the picture! The use of space and time sends important communication signals, and this chapter explores how to communicate more skillfully through your use of both space and time, and how to understand the signals others send to you.

And tenth, great communicators have an energy that is outward focused. People want to hear what they have to say, because they feel that energy when they are engaged with this person. Think of it as an invisible rainbow surrounding you. The 'colors' of this rainbow are the different aspects of who you are. These aspects include your physical self, your emotional self, your psychological self, your intellectual self, your strategic self and your spiritual self. Just as white light going through a prism separates into the colors we see in a rainbow, we can imagine your whole self being refracted into the six aspects of charisma. Some rainbows emphasize certain colors more than others do. It's the same with people and the kinds of energy they emit. As you might guess, the great communicators are the ones who emit all of their 'colors' in vibrant hues. In this chapter, I'll talk about each of these aspects and help you learn which are strongest for you, and which ones need attention.

For the rest of this chapter, I'll cover the communication process in general, but first, let's recap. I've introduced ten key qualities that are essential for becoming a great communicator. They are outward-focused energy, high adaptability, strong memory, excellent listening, skilled at asking questions as well as giving/receiving feedback, knowing how to use space and time most effectively, being good at conflict resolution, good at public presentations, and honing the power of concentration and focus. You might be thinking, "What about confidence? You can't be a great communicator without being confident." And you would be absolutely correct. However, rather than making confidence a separate quality for this book, I believe that by developing the previously mentioned ten qualities to your maximum ability, you will have the confidence that is inherent in the attitude of a great communicator. And what about vision or passion? Both are important assets to being a great communicator. I am making an assumption that anyone who takes the time and puts in the effort to develop their skills to the level of a great communicator is already passionate and has some vision for what they want to accomplish. Other traits such as gratitude come to mind, because gratitude opens up one's heart to giving and receiving the fullness of what life has to offer. Great communicators also typically have a good sense of humor. More than the ability to be witty, a good sense of humor is a protector of the soul. When you can laugh at yourself, you endear others to you. But for our purposes, I chose ten qualities that I feel reflect the characteristics of what it takes to be a great communicator and can be developed to a skill level that anyone can achieve.

Let's think for a moment about the general communication process. This includes the most common places the communication process breaks down and how you can avoid communication problems. For simplicity and practicality, I'll discuss the communication process only from your perspective. That is the only part of the process you can, and need to, control. Of course, in successful relationships, both parties participate meaningfully in the entire two-way communication process. The communication process has five basic elements: the speaker, the listener, sending, receiving, and the message.

The problem faced in any communication is how to get ideas from one person's head to another. Since we haven't figured out how to use Mr. Spock's mind-meld method of direct transfer from Star Trek, we are stuck with the problem of using an imperfect system that contains considerable opportunity for misunderstandings.

The speaker starts with what he wants to say, "the message." To send the message, he translates it into words and actions. Literally, he selects words he thinks will convey his meaning and throws in a variety of gestures and facial expressions that he believes will help transmit the message effectively (especially if he's Italian like me).

The message to be communicated is carried by the three "V elements"—verbal, vocal and visual. The words we use make up the verbal element. The vocal element includes the tone and intensity of our voice and other vocal qualities that are often referred to as the "music we play with our voice." The visual element incorporates everything that the listener can see.

Although it seems inconsistent, the most powerful element of communication is often the visual. Dynamic visual, nonverbal communication grabs and holds onto the listener's attention. Effective communication begins with getting the listener's attention through strong visual, nonverbal elements and uses powerful vocal and verbal elements to transmit the message.

On the listener's end, the message is received through a series of filters: his past experiences, his perception of the speaker, his emotional involvement with the message, his understanding of the verbal content, and his level of attention. In a sense, he translates the message into his own words, creating his own version of what he thinks the speaker was saying.

Communication problems arise in three major areas: sending the message, the environment in which the message is sent, and receiving the message.

As speakers, we don't "send" our messages perfectly. The words we choose may be ambiguous; our tone of voice may not reflect our true feelings; and our gestures may not convey the importance of the message. That means visual and vocal messages, two of the three elements of communication, can derail communication if they contradict the verbal message. Most speakers don't fully understand that the words they use are a secondary element in communication. As a matter of fact, the words used are the least important element of communication. Studies show that listeners generally attend first to the visual and then to the vocal elements of a message, finally focusing on the meaning of the words themselves.

Assume that you are a company president discussing the possibility of moving your account to a new bank. You walk into a meeting at a prospective bank where the vice-president in charge of new accounts for the bank is sitting with a messy pile of papers in front of him. His tie is stained and crooked. He sits up nervously as you walk in; his handshake is timid and his palms are sweaty. He makes very little eye contact and his eyes dart around the room frequently. His voice is squeaky and he says "uh" a lot. He mumbles. His words are, "Our bank is the best in the county. Our record for return on investment is second to none. We would really like to do business with you."

I dare you to ignore the visual information and concentrate only on the meaning of his words. The visual element is that most powerful first impression, and people respond to it before, and in spite of, the words that are spoken. The vocal elements are then processed before the actual words are heard and translated.

If the vocal sounds are bothersome or detract in any way from the meanings of the words, people will react and understand less of what was intended. Imagine a vacation-travel salesperson who speaks in a monotone voice, or an investment counselor who says, "Like . . . you know . . ." every other sentence. What if a newscaster's voice is so soft and hypnotizing that you are lulled by it? What if a speaker has a heavy regional or foreign accent? You *do* notice. You *do* respond. These sounds are recognized *before* you even get to the meaning of the words spoken.

Since visual and vocal elements are noticed before the actual words, you need to make sure your appearance and vocal tone work in harmony with your message. Look for inconsistencies such as a strong message that is delivered in a weak tone or with soft, flabby words; or a logical, fact-filled message presented in an emotional tone with ambiguous words.

Communication problems can also arise when there is too much "noise" in the environment. This "noise" creates distortions of the message and prevents it from being understood the way it was intended.

"Noise" can come from many sources, such as ringing telephones, honking horns, and messy, chaotic surroundings, all of which can prevent your message from being received clearly. Another environmental factor is time. You need to ask if the message is being delivered at an inappropriate time. Friday afternoon prior to a holiday weekend is not a good time to deliver a complicated, fact-filled report on a new marketing plan. Presenters who want their messages to be received clearly and accurately remove as much environmental noise as possible. They try to present their message in a calm, distraction-free environment at a time when the listener can devote his full attention to the message.

The message can also be garbled during reception. A word or a facial expression might be misinterpreted or a previous experience might cause the message to be translated in a way different from its intent. While communication can "break down" in several places, people who understand these problem areas have more control of the process and have fewer communication glitches.

Often, it's hard to determine the listener's ability to receive a message, which is another potential source of communication problems. The listener may be inattentive or bored. If you're presenting a message to someone who has just received either very good news or very bad news, chances are good you will be dealing with a distracted listener. The ability of a listener to receive your message is affected by his emotional state, preexisting commitments, financial pressures, and pre-judgments about you and your message. Before presenting your message, you need to make sure you have the listener's attention.

Another way of thinking about communication is to compare it to a radio station. A sender and a receiver are required to exchange the message. A powerful station can send a message to a high quality receiver and the message comes through loud and clear. A weak station trying to get a message over a range of mountains to a 1940 vacuum-tube radio doesn't have much of a chance.

There are three requirements to getting your message through clearly:

First, make sure you are a powerful station. Your words need to present your message clearly; your vocal tone needs to match and strengthen your words; and your visual appearance and gestures need to be consistent with your words and vocal tone.

Second, clear the environment. Anywhere along the process, "noise," or static, can drown out the message. Don't try to transmit over a mountain range. Eliminate distractions, excess noise, and messy, chaotic surroundings. Present your message at a time when it can be received. A radio station that wants to reach business commuters plays its message during the rush hour, not at 3:00 a.m.

And third, make sure the listener's radio is on. Get your listener's attention. Find out what frequency he's tuned to and transmit on that frequency. If he's interested in facts and figures and you're giving him emotional high drama, you're transmitting on the wrong frequency.

Anytime you hear people saying, "I didn't understand what you meant . . . I thought you said . . . You never told me . . . I didn't hear that. . . ," you know there was a failure in one of these areas and your message did not get through. We commonly call this a communication breakdown. However, you can avoid many of these breakdowns by projecting a clear verbal, vocal and visual signal in a way that gives your listener a better chance to receive it precisely as it was sent. The powerful communication processes presented here will help you develop the skills needed to filter out the noise, gain the attention of your listener and present your message in its clearest, most powerful form. I'll also help you learn how to establish a feedback process that will allow you to adjust your signal and correct errors received by your listener.

By using noise-free verbal and nonverbal skills during the sending and the feedback processes, you'll minimize communication barriers and establish an effective, efficient communication climate—a climate that establishes, maintains, and enhances mutual trust and credibility.

In the following chapters, I'll present specific verbal, vocal, and visual communication skills including: questioning, listening, and feedback, using space/time, communication adaptability, conflict resolution, energy and aura, as well as presentation, concentration and memory skills.

Of course, just hearing and learning about these skills is not enough. They need to be applied so you can increase your ability to send, listen, and give feedback to others. Therefore, in each of the following chapters I'll be describing the skills in a way that will help you not only understand the ten qualities of the world's greatest communicators; I'll help you master them.

The Art of Asking Questions

In this chapter, I will help you understand what types of questions to use and when to use them; plus I will give you some strategies and techniques of artful questioning. The fact is being able to ask the right question at the right time is a critical aspect of communicating that can easily turn a monologue into a dialogue.

You may recall in the movie "The Pink Panther," when Inspector Clouseau approached a man with a dog on a leash and asked if his dog bites. When the man said "No," Clouseau reached down to pet the dog, which promptly bit him. When he complained, saying "I thought you said your dog does not bite," the man replied, "This is not my dog."

Clouseau asked an important question about whether the man's dog bites, but failed to ask an equally important follow-up question: "Is this your dog."

Again, asking the right question at the right time is a critical piece of communicating.

The world is full of questions, good questions, silly questions, important questions, and offensive questions. Questions such as "What do you think about this project?" "Do you hope you'll win the lotto?" "What can I do to help you?" and "Are you really that stupid?"

Questions can build rapport and trust, or they can foster suspicion and dislike. They can open up a conversation and pump fresh life into it, or they can slam it closed. They truly are at the heart of interpersonal communication.

Anyone in business knows that asking good questions is particularly important in an organization. That's because working together to achieve a common purpose depends on coworkers understanding each other clearly. Their effectiveness can only be achieved by asking questions about how things are done, why they're done, who's responsible for doing them, and when they are due. Just imagine launching a new product, or putting together a budget, improving a process, implementing a new policy, or reviewing employee performance without asking any questions or even the right questions. The Information Age couldn't exist without questions.

We certainly don't need to be taught to ask questions. The average three-year old asks 4.2 questions per minute. Then, when we reach school age, our education system takes great pains to teach us to ask questions, in particular, "Why?" Everyone assumes we know all we need to know about asking questions by the time we've learned what a question mark is. After all, that's what a question is, right? It's a group of words followed by a question mark. Well, that may be the definition of a question, but comparing that to the *art* of asking questions is like saying that if you can spell "car" you're ready for the Indy 500.

The art of asking questions is just that—an art. So we'll dig a little deeper to help you develop this skill that will empower your communication skills. We'll start by *answering* a question, which is "*Why* do we ask questions?"

The standard response to this is "Because we want to know something." And it's true—questions are a powerful tool for getting information. In fact, they are the heart of gathering information, which is why we ask questions like Who? What? Where? When? Why? How? and How much?

However questioning has a much richer payoff than just gaining information. Questions can also be used for many other reasons. Here are a few of the reasons:

They can stimulate conversation. Imagine attending a social function where no one could ask a question! You couldn't ask, "What have you been up to?" Or, "Have you heard such and such?" Or you couldn't ask if someone saw a particular movie or what he or she thought of it. It would be a pretty strange gathering, and pretty dull.

Questions can be used to learn other people's views. Think how often you ask questions that start with "What do you think about . . ." Or "Can you tell me how you feel about. . . ?" We've learned that when we need to know what someone else is thinking or feeling, we can ask very direct questions.

Or how about this use of questions: **to check to see if someone is in agreement with you.** If you're wondering what someone thinks about what you've been discussing you ask questions like:

- "Do you think we're on the right track?"
- "Can you support this decision?" or
- "Do you have any concerns?"

Building rapport and trust can be achieved by asking questions when they show support for the other person's goals and objectives. In this case, you find yourself asking things like:

- "How can I help you?"
- "What would you like to accomplish?" or
- "Tell me about your goals, dreams, or objectives."

Finally, you can use questions to **verify the information you heard.** This can be very important; because I'm sure you've been in a situation where what you initially thought you heard was not what was meant. Asking for feedback is a critical part of the communication process. That's why we ask questions that start with "Did I understand you to mean . . . ? or "Is this a fair way to summarize what you said?

So there are many reasons *why* we ask questions. But there are only two basic types of questions: closed and open. Each type is very important to the communication process.

Closed questions are generally simple, information-gathering questions. The response to this type of question is usually "yes," "no," or a very brief answer.

Here are some examples of closed questions:

"What time is it?" "Did you finish the project?" "Are you going to the meeting?" and "When did you first discover the problem?" As you can see, they are generally easy to answer and seldom intimidating.

Closed questions perform many functions. For example, they allow specific facts to be gathered. We ask questions like "What color do you prefer?"

They're useful in the feedback process when someone wants to check the accuracy or completeness of the communication. You'll hear questions such as "Do I have the correct information?"

Closed questions can be used to gain commitment to a position. You would ask, "Does this seem right so far?"

If you want to reinforce positive statements, you'd use a closed question such as "This seems like a good plan, doesn't it?"

This type of question is useful for directing a conversation to a desired topic. You would ask "Do you have time to talk about the budget?"

These are some of the functions of closed questions. Now, let's look at **open questions**.

When asked this type of question, people generally provide longer, more complete answers. Open questions are used to draw out a wide range of responses on a broad topic and often ask for opinions, thoughts or feelings. Here are some typical open questions:

- "How did you feel about the meeting?"
- "What could we do to make this project better?"
- "How can we meet our objectives?" and
- "How important is it to you?"

Open questions have the following characteristics:

They can't be answered by a simple "yes" or "no." Here's an open question: "How do you think we could make this process work better?" That's in contrast to "*Do* you think we could do this process better?" which could be answered by "yes" or "no."

Generally, open questions begin with "what" or "how." For example, "What do you think about the new benefit policy?"

Open questions do not lead the answer. An example of leading would be this: "How much do you like our neat new marketing plan?" An open question along this same line would be "Where could we make improvements, if any, in the new marketing plan?"

You would use an open question to draw out ideas and feelings. Such as, "How do you feel about the reorganization of the department?"

Open questions encourage elaboration on objectives, needs, wants and problems, and they promote self-discovery. A director at a company might ask, "How do you think the new process will work for your group?"

I'll give you two more characteristics of open questions. One, they stimulate thinking. And two, they allow a broad range of responses. Think of the varied answers to the question, "How would you change the policy to make it better?"

It's important to know which kind of question, open or closed, to use to enhance communications. Both are useful and can help you achieve several different purposes, including fact-finding, feeling finding, clarifying, expanding, and directing. Let's look at each one.

If you're looking for specific information and data, in other words, fact-finding, you'll want to use a question that asks for the detail you need. Consider how the question, "What did you accomplish on the project?" will generate a more detailed answer than "Did you get a lot done?"

When you're feeling-finding, that is, wanting to understand a person's feeling about a subject, you'll generally ask open questions. The closed question, "Are you happy about the project?" doesn't get the same response as the open question: "How do you feel about the project?" Used properly, feeling-finding questions generate a lot of information about attitudes, convictions, and motivations. This type of question is extremely powerful because it is so seldom asked, and sadly, the answers are listened to carefully even less frequently.

Closed questions are used to verify and clarify your understanding of a conversation.

- "Did I understand you to say. . . ?"
- "Are you referring to. . . ?"
- "Do you mean. . . ?"

These are examples of questions you can ask to make sure you understand the information someone is giving you.

Open questions are useful for expanding or drawing out further information on a topic. To do this, you'd ask questions like

- "Can you give me an example?"
- "Would you tell me more about that point?"
- "What else might be causing a problem?"

These types of questions generate more information about a subject.

Directing questions are generally closed questions that are used to point the conversation toward a particular goal. Here are some examples:

- "What was the other point you wanted to make?"
- "Can we go back and talk about your first item?"
- "Couldn't we postpone the decision for a week?"

These types of questions direct the conversation to a different topic or lead the person to a particular decision.

Understanding the different types of questions is one thing. Using them effectively requires having a strategy. The truth is, all forms of communication can be improved by planning and understanding the focus of the communication, and questioning is certainly no exception. If you intend to ask someone a question, you should know what you're trying to accomplish by asking the question. If you're trying to find out how someone feels about an upcoming change, slapping them on the back and saying, "Sounds great, doesn't it?" will probably not meet your goals. Too often people think they're asking a question for one reason when they really want something else.

A chemistry professor tells the story about his 5-year old son who stopped him in their kitchen one day and asked how the refrigerator worked. The professor was pleased that his son was interested in the workings of this mechanical device and launched into a lecture about how a particular gas inside the refrigerator tubing is compressed and then cools when expanded. As he began citing the formula that describes this heat exchange, his son interrupted and asked, "Can I have a Popsicle?" That's when the professor finally realized what his son had actually wanted all along.

Asking the wrong question is probably something we've all been guilty of. For example, if you ask someone what they think about a new budget, you may actually want to know if they'll support it. A question such as "Is there anything in the budget you couldn't support?" would do a better job of giving you the feedback you're looking for.

One of the most fundamental questioning techniques is to start with broad, open questions and then build on the responses by asking narrower, more specific questions. This is called the funnel technique. It's like painting a picture. You start with a blank canvas and begin filling in the background with broad-brush strokes. Gradually, you add more and more detail until you have a complete picture. With questions, you start out at the top of the funnel with a broad question and then as you move down the funnel, you "paint with a finer brush" by asking closed questions that give you more exact answers. This fills in the details.

With the funnel technique, you can explore the other person's needs and expectations, problems and opportunities by using your questioning and listening skills. You start with general questions like, "Tell me about your business" or "What are your long range goals in this position?" A typical computer salesperson might ask a prospect what kind of computer system they currently have or what their computer needs are. The hotshot salesperson who has learned the funnel technique starts out at a higher level by asking about the prospect's business or operation. Similarly, a manager trying to locate the cause of a recurring problem could say "Why does this switch keep failing?" An artful questioning manager would start on a broader level saying something like, "Tell me about the overall process that surrounds the switch." A supervisor trying to deal with a tardy employee could ask why the employee is late again. Or he could sit down with the employee and ask, "How are you feeling about your job?" Broad-brush questions give you a lot of information about the situation, including important clues that lead to more specific follow-up questions. A side benefit is they give the other person a chance to relax and tell you what's important.

Another benefit to broad, open-ended questions is they show your interest in the other person's situation.

They often start with "tell me," "how," "who," "what," or "why." They're much more powerful than closed questions that require a simple answer such as "yes" or "no" or a specific piece of information. After the broad question opens the conversation and begins to build rapport, the artful questioner builds on the responses to gain more understanding. Our computer salesperson might have a client who says, "I need more control over our order system." He then builds on that response by asking a question using the most important words in the answer—control and order system. For instance, he might ask, "What aspects of your order system would you like to have more control over?" or "Could you tell me more about your order system?" When the client responds, he bases his next question around that response, building his understanding of the client's need with each question and response.

One of the reasons the funnel technique is so effective is that the broad, open questions at the top of the funnel are easy for people to answer. They have the freedom to tell you whatever they want. By the time you get to the more specific questions, they can see where you're heading and be willing to share more information with you. Not only that, most people's level of trust and willingness to share information is related directly to how much information they have previously shared.

Here's an example of building on previous responses. Imagine two people meeting on an airplane. After some small talk, one person asks the other what she does for a living. Her response is, "I'm a writer." A natural follow up question would be, "A *writer* . . . what kind of writing do you do?" The answer might be something like "Mostly humor. Occasionally I write something serious or philosophical but people seem to laugh at that, too." Digging deeper into this response, I would say something like, "I've always thought humor must be the hardest kind of writing to do. Tell me how you do it." This intelligent use of the funnel technique now opens the door for a fairly in-depth conversation. This technique guides it from a simple, non-meaningful declaration of, "I'm a writer," to a fairly detailed, very personal expression.

Here are some general strategies to help you formulate your questions in a way that helps you meet your objectives in any particular situation.

For starters, have a plan. You need to know what you want to accomplish and what type of questions you'll need to use. Of course, you don't have to have the questions written out in advance, but you should be clear about your objectives.

Next, keep the questions simple. What I mean by that is it's best to ask for one answer at a time. A question like, "What do you think about the marketing plan and will the new ad campaign confuse customers and would that confusion actually be detrimental to the long-term product growth?" will not give you a meaningful answer. If you ask a multi-part question, people tend to either answer only the last part, or only the part they're interested in or feel safe with. So, one question at a time!

Another part of an overall strategy is to stay focused. You'll want to keep the questions on track and following a topic to its conclusion. Any question that starts with "By the way" is probably going off on a tangent. Hold that question for later.

A fourth tip is to stay non-threatening. As I'm sure you've experienced, trust is essential in communication. The wrong question can quickly destroy trust and the relationship you've built. Questions that begin with "Why didn't you. . . ?" or "How could you. . . ?" generally make people defensive. Once someone throws up a wall, the opportunity for gathering information and building a relationship quickly goes away.

Next, make it a habit of asking permission. This is especially important if the area of questioning is sensitive. It's always best to explain the need for the questions and ask permission before proceeding. For example, if someone is applying for a loan or perhaps a club membership, they'll be asked, "The application requires some detail about your financial condition. Would you mind answering a few questions?"

Avoiding ambiguity is another important strategy. Let's be honest. Ambiguous questions generate ambiguous answers. Asking "*Could* you support the budget?" doesn't tell you whether the person *would* support it.

And finally, avoid manipulation. This means keeping the relationship a primary focus. If you trick someone into giving you an answer you want, you could easily destroy trust and rapport. The question, "Would you prefer to work overtime tonight or tomorrow night?" doesn't give a person the chance to say he doesn't want to work overtime at all. By first explaining the need for the overtime and then asking if he's available has a totally different feel. Manipulation is an attempt to take away the other person's control. Don't do it! Not if you are interested in gaining truthful and accurate information to your questions. Mastering the art of asking questions helps you gain the information you need, build trust, stimulate the views and opinions of others, and verify information. And that is the goal any great communicator.

The Power
of Listening

The power of listening is one of those skills where the lack of it can have as much of a negative effect as having it can create positive effects.

Ineffective listening is one of the most frequent causes of lost sales and customers, misunderstandings, mistakes, and jobs that need to be redone. Managers who are poor listeners often miss the essence of the message being sent, leading them to propose solutions that are faulty or inappropriate. Inevitably, employees stop listening when the manager isn't listening, which creates the potential for organizational disaster.

Following any major problem, there will always be one or more people who say, "I tried to tell them." Studies of the Space Shuttle Challenger tragedy show that there may have been as many as 1100 people who knew about the potential danger of failure of the O-ring, which caused the catastrophic explosion. A responsive listening organization might have heard the warnings in time to stop the disaster.

It is no different in people's private lives. Poor listening skills lead the breakdown in relationships, whether it is divorce or a divide between a parent and child.

With all these negative consequences, why don't we listen more effectively? Here are five basic reasons.

First, listening is hard work because it is more than just keeping quiet. It's focusing on the other person rather than on ourselves and as a result, many people just don't do it.

Next is competition. We are bombarded with so much incoming stimuli, such as radio, TV, movies, pop-ups, advertisements and texts, and we have learned not to pay close attention to information that seems irrelevant. But that means sometimes we screen out things that *are* important. The consequences can be tragic. Four months before the 9/11 attacks, three different workers at Logan Airport reported suspicious activity around a security gate. A man, who turned out to be one of the future hijackers, was videotaping and photographing the checkpoint. Unfortunately, the warnings to security officials were ignored even though two months previously, federal authorities had advised airlines that al Qaeda terrorists typically conducted surveillance before attacking a target. If the suspicious behavior had been taken seriously, rather than screened out as irrelevant, the results of 9/11 could possibly have been very different.

Another roadblock to effective listening is that we rush to action. We think we know what someone is going to say, and we want to act on that person's words. So, we jump in and interrupt, not taking the time to listen and hear the person out.

Next, a listening gap caused by the difference in our speaking speed and listening speed causes a hindrance to being a good listener. The average person speaks at about 135-175 words a minute, but can listen to 400-500 words a minute. For poor listeners, that time gap is filled with jumping to conclusions, daydreaming, planning a reply, or mentally arguing with the speaker.

Not surprisingly, a lack of training keeps us from developing better listening skills. This is ironic since we spend more time listening than speaking, reading, or writing. Yet, most receive almost no formal education in listening.

The normal, untrained listener is likely to understand and retain only about 50 percent of a conversation. Forty-eight hours later, this already poor percentage drops to an even more dismal retention rate of 25 percent. This means the details of a particular conversation that took place more than a couple of days before will always be incomplete and usually inaccurate. It's no wonder people can seldom agree about what has been discussed!

Needless-to-say, improvement in an activity as simple as listening can have such a powerful impact on an organization.

In fact, many years ago, a team of professors at Loyola University in Chicago participated in a study to determine the most important single attribute of an effective manager. After studying hundreds of businesses across the country, they concluded that listening is a manager's most important skill.

Here's a recap of some of the benefits of better listening:

- You can improve your relationships. When you listen to somebody, it makes them feel good about you, which leads to increased trust and credibility, plus an increased willingness to cooperate.
- You'll have fewer misunderstandings. In business settings, fewer errors results in lower costs, better products and services, and higher profits.
- And, better listening also leads to better understanding, which improves the transfer of information, develops teamwork, builds morale, and leads to higher productivity.

The key is to become an *Active Listener*, which is unquestionably the most comprehensive, and potentially the most powerful form of listening. Not surprisingly, it's also the most demanding and tiring. This is because it requires the deepest level of concentration, attention and mental, as well as emotional, processing effort.

The active listener refrains from coming to judgment about the speaker's message, and instead focuses on understanding the other person's point of view. Attention is concentrated on the thoughts and feelings of the speaker, in addition to the words spoken. Listening in this manner requires initial suspension of our personal thoughts and feelings in order to give attention solely to the message and intent of the speaker. It means figuratively "putting yourself into someone else's shoes." It also requires that the listener send verbal and nonverbal feedback to the speaker indicating that what is being said is actually being absorbed.

In order to develop this highest level of listening proficiency, you need to develop six separate skills. I've combined them into an easy-to-remember model that forms the word CARESS. Each letter stands for a step that will help you become an active listener whether you are listening to a keynote speaker, your boss, your co-workers, a friend, or family members:

- **Concentrate.** You need to focus your attention on the speaker and only on the speaker.
- **Acknowledge.** There is power in acknowledging the speaker.
- **Research.** Active listeners gather information about speakers by asking them questions.
- **Exercising emotional control.** This needs to be done regardless of how provocative the message is, which means concentrating on understanding it first.
- **Sense** the nonverbal message. You should be analyzing what the speaker is saying with his body language and gestures.
- **Structure.** Active listeners structure or organize the information as they receive it. This is what should be done during the time generated by the gap between speaking and hearing speeds.

Let's take them one by one.

The first step in active listening is to **concentrate** completely on the speaker. It is the job of the listener to eliminate noise and distractions because they can be a barrier, totally eliminating your ability to listen. If you don't concentrate, you don't hear. And if you don't hear, you certainly cannot listen. Concentration and focus is such a critical skill of both listening and communicating that I've made it one of the ten qualities of the world's greatest communicators and we will cover it in more detail later.

The second step is to **acknowledge** the speaker, which shows that you are listening and interested in their message. This acknowledgment encourages the speaker and actually helps them to send a clearer message. To understand how to acknowledge a speaker, think about how *you* like to be listened to.

What are the most important things you like to see in another person when they're listening to you? Here are four things most people mention:

- Eye contact.
- Verbal responses and participation such as asking questions and vocal prompts.
- Non-verbal gestures such as smiling, nodding of the head, and leaning forward with interest.
- Seeking to clarify by asking questions or paraphrasing the speaker's points to make sure they were accurately received.

When you acknowledge the speaker, you're letting the speaker know the message is being received. You are giving positive feedback that you are interested in what's being said and that you understand the message.

The third step is **research**. In most contexts this means getting information out of books or online. But as a listening skill, research is what you do to keep the conversation a two-way flow of communication, by asking questions and making clarifying or empathy statements. This two-way flow facilitates a meeting of the minds between the speaker and the listener in the way it allows you to clarify a message, enlarge upon a subject, or go into a particular topic in more depth.

Skillful research simplifies the listener's job because it gets the speaker to "open up" and reveal inner feelings, motives, needs, goals, and desires.

It also allows you to get the speaker to change the direction of the conversation or prompt the speaker to "vent" feelings of anger, excitement, and enthusiasm. Research also allows you to support and reinforce particular parts of a speaker's message.

Another technique of research is to use empathy statements. These consist of three specific parts, a tentative statement, defining the speaker's feeling, and putting it into its situational context.

An example of an empathy statement would be, "It seems to me you're very frustrated because you can't get the product to work the way you want it to work." The phrase "it seems to me" is what makes it a tentative statement. The phrase "you're very frustrated" attempts to define the speaker's feeling. And finally, the phrase "because you can't get the product to work the way you want it to work" puts it into its situational context—the situation that caused the person to experience the feeling of frustration.

Empathy statements get people to open up and share their feelings and thoughts with you. The reason they work so well is that by rephrasing the speaker's message as an empathy statement, it not only proves that you're paying attention, it provides encouragement for the speaker and is non-judgmental. In addition, it gives the speaker an opportunity to refine, expand or correct the message. By affirming the speaker's feelings, empathy statements help build an emotional bond between the speaker and the listener and this is an essential part of active listening.

The next step in CARESS is **exercising emotional control**. In order to develop this skill, try to understand what causes an emotional overreaction. It's generally prompted by something about the speaker or has something to do with what the speaker says. It can be caused by differences in values, beliefs, attitudes, education, the speed of delivery, an image, or a host of other things. What these have in common is they cause a disruption in communication between the speaker and the listener.

The speaker may have certain dress or speech patterns, or other idiosyncrasies, that may totally turn off the listener or cause the listener to receive the speaker's message negatively. For instance, going to a bank for a loan dressed in overly casual clothing might negatively influence the bank manager's opinion on your credit worthiness. On the other hand, wearing a high-powered Wall Street suit might put a rural businessperson on the defensive against a not-to-be trusted city slicker.

A person's accent can cause an emotional reaction in the listener. For instance, there's no doubt that many people make value judgments about the intelligence of a person with a Brooklyn accent versus someone with a New England accent.

Loaded words can also often cause a severe emotional over-reaction. Whenever a speaker uses ethnic, racial, religious, or political words or inappropriate humor, it's likely to cause an emotional reaction in many listeners.

If, as listeners we fall prey to focusing on the provocative aspects of a speaker, we can miss the true substance of what is being said. When we exercise emotional control, we can avoid blocking the meaning of the speaker's message. This is done by first recognizing and then redirecting your negative emotional reactions.

We can recognize the beginning of an emotional overreaction by noticing when you're getting upset about something. As an emotional overreaction begins, there is an almost irresistible tendency to interrupt, to butt in, and to argue. Recognizing this urge is the first step in controlling the response.

Then, you can redirect your negative emotional reaction with the following techniques. You can pause and delay your response. Then, try to think about what you have in common, rather than focusing on what's different. And third, imagine yourself calm and relaxed. Controlling emotional reactions empowers you to become an effective listener even when the message is delivered in what could be a polarizing context.

The fifth major component of active listening is **sensing**, which focuses on the non-verbal communications of body language and vocal intonations.

Body language is certainly not a new phenomenon. People have known about it and used it since the beginning of time. Even before language was developed as a communications tool, body language was used to make needs and desires known to others. It encompasses everything from the subtlest raising of an eyebrow to the precise movements of the sophisticated sign language used by the deaf.

Some gestures are even more expressive than words. Picture a person slapping his forehead, accompanied by an audible groan. Doesn't this suggest that he just remembered something he was supposed to do? Implicit in this gesture is a rebuke to himself for his oversight.

Other well-known gestures are saluting, tipping one's hat, shaking hands, shrugging shoulders, waving good-bye, forming an "OK" with thumb and forefinger, and blowing a kiss.

The ability to understand body language is apparently not related to IQ, the ability to take tests, or the grades one gets in school. Study and practice tends to improve your ability to understand body language.

We have a plethora of courses and seminars that teach us how to write and speak better, but there are relatively few available in the study of nonverbal communications and body language.

Sigmund Freud, an early believer in the utility of body language, distrusted the spoken word and based much of his work on the assumption that words hide more than they reveal. Freud believed, as do many researchers, that although we cannot rely on the truth of words, nonverbal behavior often does project truth.

In fact, body language is often more reliable than verbal communication and may even contradict verbal expressions. It's appears to be an outlet for feelings and can function as a lie detector to aid a watchful observer in interpreting words.

Interestingly, vocal intonation is a form of nonverbal communication in that it can convey a meaning apart from the words that are being spoken. Vocal intonation is that part of the meaning that can be lost when speech is written rather than spoken. This is unfortunate since the verbal and vocal parts of messages do not always communicate the same meaning or feeling. Simple changes in voice qualities can change the meaning or emotion of the same group of words from one thing to another. A good example is sarcasm, where the information being transmitted vocally has quite a different meaning from what is being transmitted verbally. Consider the statement, said sincerely, "Well good for you" versus the sarcastically delivered "Well good for you."

By simple changes in vocal qualities, we can convey totally separate and unique feelings and emotions. A lack of emotional sensitivity to voice tones can create communication problems. The primary thing to look for when you pay attention to voice intonations, are changes in the voice qualities of the person you're listening to. Another good example is how many vocal versions we can use for the word "oh"—I understand, I don't understand, surprise, disappointment, disgust, affection.

Some people naturally speak slowly, loudly, or clearly. When these people change their normal voice qualities, they're communicating something extra. It's up to you to know these vocal qualities, and to notice when they're changing. Then, and only then, can you react to these changes.

Here are the seven major vocal qualities:

- Resonance is the ability of one's voice to fill a space. It's an intensification and enrichment of the voice tone.
- Rhythm is the flow, pace, and movement of the voice.
- Speed is how fast or slow the voice is used.
- Pitch is affected by the tightening or relaxing of the vocal cords—it's the highness or lowness of sound.
- Volume is the degree of loudness or intensity of the voice.
- Inflection is the change in pitch or volume of the voice.
- Clarity is the crisp articulation and enunciation of the words.

The way someone says something can have a great effect on what meaning is being communicated. This is why it is important for listeners and speakers to learn what different voice intonations mean, how to identify them, and how to use them effectively to get their message across. Studies have shown that although a manager may speak the same words to three different employees individually, his or her feelings and biases toward each employee are clearly projected non-verbally, in vocal intonation as well as body language. And although the manager is not aware of this subconscious, non-verbal messaging, it is clearly communicated to and identified by the employees.

By learning more about vocal behavior and voice intonations, you'll have a much better idea of the true feelings and intent of the people you're talking to. In addition, you'll have a better understanding of how others perceive you through your voice intonations.

Structuring is the last segment of the "CARESS" formula. This is where we listen primarily to the verbal component—the content—of somebody's message. As I explained earlier, there's a time gap created by the difference in listening and speaking speeds. We can use this time to structure the message we're listening to. This revolves around taking mental or written notes of the topic or the major idea. Structuring is focusing on the key points being discussed, as well as the reasons, sub points, and supporting points.

There are transitional words and phrases speakers use that make indexing easier for us to do. A phrase such as "What I want to talk to you about today is...." will clearly be followed by what is probably the main idea, the subject, or the topic. Then, key points can be indexed when you hear someone begin sections with numbers, like "first," "second, "third" and so on. This speaker is making it easy to stay plugged in and indexing helps. Additionally, phrases like "for example," or "let me elaborate on that," generally tells you that a rationale, a sub point, or a supporting point is likely to follow.

The second primary activity of structuring is sequencing. This is listening for order or priority. Sometimes, someone tells you something where the order is very important, or you're being given instructions or directions where the order is crucial. In sequencing, as in indexing, you want to listen for transitional words like "first," "second," "third," etc. If you have any doubt or confusion, check with the speaker with a comment such as, "Let me make sure I understand what should be done first," or "Let me make sure I understand the priority of your needs." Feedback and clarification will help you get the proper sequence.

These are the six major skills needed to practice active listening. But equally important to learning and implementing these skills, is the harder task of developing the active listening attitude. You do this by first understanding that listening is as powerful as speech.

A second attitude you need to develop is that listening saves time. People who listen actively find that they experience fewer mistakes, fewer interpersonal misunderstandings, less employee and customer turnover, and fewer false starts. We can better develop positive long-term relationships by actively listening to each other.

A third and final attitude you need to acquire is that listening is important and worthwhile with everyone. When you believe you can learn something from everyone you meet, I guarantee you'll approach listening with a completely new enthusiasm.

The payoff for improving the skill of listening is enormous. As an active listener, you'll have fewer communication glitches, your relationships will improve, and productivity and morale will go up in your organization as well as your home. However, while listening skills are simple, they are not particularly easy to implement. For most of us, it means breaking a lifetime of poor listening habits.

Using the CARESS model can help you break through this barrier of poor listening. As you begin to *Concentrate-Acknowledge-Research-Exercise Emotional Control-Sense the Nonverbal Message-and Structure the Content of the Message*, your ability to accurately receive the messages sent to you will improve. And that is a major step in becoming a great communicator.

Feedback

The third quality of the World's Greatest Communicators is Feedback. This communication quality is often taken for granted. It may very well be the most important aspect of interpersonal communications if a conversation is to continue for any length of time and still have meaning for the parties involved. After all, without feedback, how does each person really know what the other person is talking about and communicating?

For instance, what do the following phrases mean to you?

- "In a little while."
- "I'll be there in a minute."
- "It isn't very far." or
- "Let's get together sometime."

I'm sure you realized that most, if not all, of these statements are highly ambiguous. When they're used in normal conversation, there's a high probability they will be misinterpreted, unless they are clarified. For example, when someone says: "Call me later and we'll discuss it," do they mean fifteen minutes from now, one hour from now, tomorrow, or next week? This statement, along with thousands of others, can have a variety of meanings, and therefore generate misunderstandings.

Unfortunately, we frequently use these statements in everyday conversation and expect the other person to understand what we mean. Instead, they create errors, misunderstandings, and strained relationships. However, through the simple use of feedback skills, these highly ambiguous statements can be transformed into specific, effective communications.

In the workplace, a lack of feedback can cause errors, and botched plans, political in-fighting, lost productivity, lost profits, and ultimately, lost jobs. In fact, studies show that the lack of clear communication is a major factor in just about every organizational problem. Conversely, feedback and clarification can take the ambiguity out of promises, agreements, schedules, policies, and procedures.

Let's take a look at the feedback skills you can use to make sure your message is clear to the people with whom you communicate, whether it's your colleagues, supervisors, employees, contractors, customers, or friends and family.

Feedback comes in a number of forms, including verbal feedback, nonverbal feedback, fact feedback, and feeling feedback. Each one serves a specific purpose in the communications process.

We'll start with **Verbal Feedback**, where you can accomplish a number of things. You can use it to ask for clarification of a message or to give positive or negative strokes to the other person. It can be used to determine how to structure a presentation that will be meaningful and effective for the other person.

To help improve the accuracy and clarity of a message during a conversation, you could use statements such as these:

- "Let me be sure I understand what you've said."
- "Let's see if I can review the key points we've discussed."
- "As I understand it, your major objectives are . . ."

Using feedback for clarification is probably the most critical use of feedback in the workplace. There's really only one way to know if the message you're receiving is the one intended, and that is by asking for clarification, or restating the message in your own words and asking for verification that you understand it. Obviously, you can't clarify or verify everything that is said during the day. If your co-worker says he's going to get a cup of coffee and you ask for clarification, the results you get probably will not be positive. You need to know when to use feedback. Typical times would be when you have any doubt about the meaning of the message or about how to proceed, or when the message is highly complex. You'd also want feedback when you're dealing with an important process or project, and when the message deals with information that is new to you or must take place in a particular sequence.

Verbal feedback should also be used to give positive and negative strokes to others. When a person does something positive, that behavior needs to be positively reinforced. This can be done through simple statements, such as:

- "The project report you did was clear and concise—nice job."
- "You made it really easy for the committee to understand the issues."
- "I really appreciate the extra effort you put in."

For it to be most effective, tell the person specifically what you recognize and appreciate.

Given in a timely and consistent manner, this type of feedback lets the person know what kind of performance is required, and it encourages them to continue with similar performance.

On the other hand, when behavior requires negative feedback, offer it in a private, constructive environment. By all means, don't ignore it! This tends to prolong inappropriate performance since silence is viewed as tacit approval. Of course, no one likes to be criticized, so negative feedback should be directed only at the performance, not at the person. And whenever possible, negative feedback should be sandwiched between positive feedback.

Here are some examples of this:

- "It's obvious you put in a lot of effort on this report. However, the issues are so complex it would help if we had a one-page summary."

- "Your work is extremely accurate but when you come in late, it puts us all behind schedule."
- "I appreciate your help folding the brochures. Since they'll be going to customers, it's important they're extremely neat. Could you redo these?"

The key here is to give the person enough specific information so they can correct their performance in the future.

Getting feedback during a presentation is also vitally important. By asking simple questions, you can determine whether it's working and if you should continue in the current direction or if you should modify your approach.

For instance, if you think you're going a bit too fast for the other person to comprehend, you might simply ask: "I sometimes get carried away with my enthusiasm and move too quickly on this topic. Would it be more helpful to you if I covered these issues a bit more slowly?" The same can be done if you're getting the impression you should speed up your presentation. A good question would be, "Should we explore this issue some more, or should we move on?" This allows you to determine the other person's interest and understanding of the conversation. Their answers can help you avoid capriciously cutting the topic too short or, perhaps worse, dragging it on too long. You're simply asking for direction. By asking "Would you like me to go into the details of this project, or do you have some other questions that you'd like to ask me first?" allows you to gauge the person's present state of mind and level of receptivity. Without this information, you may get into the details of the project when, in fact, the other person has questions that should be answered first. In this situation, people tend to dwell on their questions and stop paying attention to what you're explaining. Through these types of questions, you can tailor your delivery style and presentation to fit the needs of each individual person. Although it's true this takes a bit more time in the short run, in the end, it saves more time because it prevents communication problems and improves receptivity, understanding, and productivity.

Now let's turn our attention to **Nonverbal Feedback**. Many of us can remember when the word "vibes" was in vogue. Both good and bad vibes are the result of a direct form of nonverbal feedback. People use their bodies, eyes, faces, postures, and senses, to communicate a variety of positive or negative attitudes, feelings, and opinions. We all do this consciously and unconsciously, but the sensitive, perceptive communicator uses this nonverbal feedback to structure the content and direction of their message. As a result, the interaction stays positive and on track, while trust and credibility is increased. I learned as a professional keynote speaker to read the nonverbal feedback of the audience to monitor and determine the pace and content of my presentation.

Here's an important thing to remember. The amount of nonverbal feedback you receive and send is not as important as how you interpret it and react to it. These nonverbal signals help you realize when you are losing the other person's interest. When you are sensitive to the nonverbal feedback that is communicating this loss of interest, you can react by changing your pace, topic, or style to recapture the person's (or in my case, the audience's) attention and interest.

As you can imagine, nonverbal feedback is extremely important in the manager/employee relationship. Too often, ineffective communications between managers and employees result in "mixed messages." This simply means that while one message is being verbalized, something totally different is being stated through nonverbal feedback, such as vocal intonation and body language. When a person receives mixed messages, it immediately creates tension and distrust. Right or wrong, they feel something is purposely being hidden from them. Adding to the tension, they are forced to choose between the verbal message and the nonverbal message being communicated by body language, and most often, they choose the nonverbal message. Unfortunately, managers and employees often don't realize they are sending mixed messages to each other. The miscommunication it produces takes a terrible toll on work relationships. That is why it is extremely important to keep your nonverbal feedback and your verbal feedback in sync.

Another very important type of feedback is **Fact Feedback**. You want this when you are relating specific information that needs to be received as accurately as possible. To get this feedback, you ask specific, closed-ended questions, or make a specific statement of the facts as you know them and then ask for verification. This type of feedback gives you clarification, agreement, or correction about the facts.

Fact feedback is also used in translating messages and interpreting words or phrases. The following messages contain words or phrases that are unclear, which makes then perfect candidates for fact feedback.

Consider this statement: "Due to recent layoffs, all employees are expected to work harder."

A request for fact feedback would be: "What exactly do you mean by 'working harder?' Should we plan on putting in longer hours?"

Here's statement we've all heard that can have a wide range of meanings: "There will be a short wait for a table."

A logical fact feedback question would be: "How long is the wait? Will the wait be more than 15 minutes?" Of course, we know it will be more than 15 minutes!

Or here's one more: "Don't spend too much time on that job."

This would prompt the question: "Just how much time should I spend on the job? Is there a deadline?"

The point is, if something can be misunderstood, chances are it will be misunderstood. Use fact feedback to keep your messages clear and make sure you're receiving the message as it is intended.

We have looked at Verbal, Non-verbal, and Fact Feedback. Now we will consider one more: **Feeling Feedback.** Through the first three types,

Verbal, Nonverbal, and Fact Feedback, we may have gained a firm understanding and clarification of the words, phrases, and facts of a message. However, this increased accuracy still only stays on the surface of the communication. It is also important to know *why* the person is saying the things she is saying. What are the underlying causes and motivations behind her message and her facts? How much personal feeling does her message carry for her? All these questions underscore the importance of seeking feeling feedback in two-way communications.

Feeling feedback is especially important in organizations, perhaps because it's so seldom asked for. The old school of business believed that feelings had no place in the workplace, and that personal lives, feelings and emotional involvements were to be taken care of outside of the workplace. But that has changed. We now know it's impossible to put our feelings in a little box as we walk into the office and then pick them up as we leave. This is borne out by research that shows one of the most effective ways to handle organizational change is to let the people "chat" about how they *feel* about the change. Just the process of talking about their feelings, helps them adapt.

Feeling feedback should be two-directional. On the one hand, you need to make a concerted effort to understand the feelings and attitudes that underlie the messages coming to you. Conversely, you should clearly project feeling feedback to the person communicating to you, so that person knows their message has gotten through to you, especially at the feeling level.

The following statements are candidates for feeling feedback questions:

- "I'm tired of all the politics around here."
- "My last review was a joke."
- "No one cares about my problems."

Examples of requests for feeling feedback to these statements would be:

- "How are the politics here affecting you?"
- "What's bothering you about your last review?"
- "What would make you feel like the organization cared about your problems?"

If we compare feeling feedback to fact feedback, the latter is simply a meeting of the minds, whereas feeling feedback is a meeting of the hearts. Feeling feedback is nothing more than effectively putting yourself into other people's shoes so you can see things from their viewpoints. When you can really experience another person's true feelings and understand where they are coming from, and at the same time project this emotional awareness to the person, it serves to reinforce rapport, lower interpersonal tension, and significantly increase trust. The key tools you use to send and receive feeling feedback are probing questions, supportive and understanding responses, and an awareness and projection of appropriate nonverbal signals. It's important to use these tools effectively since understanding the feelings inherent in a message are just as important as understanding the facts. The truth is, quite often, until you and the other person understand how each other truly feels, the "facts" don't matter at all. Great communicators improve the accuracy of communications through fact feedback, and improve the rapport of their relationships by practicing empathy through feeling feedback.

If you took a few moments and really thought about it, you could probably recall numerous times where you could have smoothed over problems in communication simply by using the forms of feedback I've discussed here. I do, of course, understand that effective communication between two people is not easy. You really have to practice to make it work. The proper use of questioning skills helps along with using active listening. Sensitivity to nonverbal behavior helps. But without feedback, all of these skills are less effective. Through the effective use of feedback skills, you can greatly improve your communications. Following are several general guidelines that will help you use your feedback skills more effectively.

First, it's important to give and get definitions. The interpretation of words or phrases may vary from person to person, group to group, and region to region. When people believe or assume that words are used for one and only one meaning, they create situations in which they think they understand others but really don't. The words you use in everyday conversations almost inevitably have multiple meanings. In fact, the 500 most commonly used words in our language have more than 14,000 dictionary definitions. For instance, according to

Webster, a person is considered "fast" when they can run rather quickly. However, when one is tied down and cannot move at all, this is also considered "fast." "Fast" also relates to periods of not eating, a ship's mooring line, and a racetrack in good running condition.

This abundance of meanings of even "simple" words makes it hazardous to assume to understand the intent of a message without verifying and clarifying that message. These assumptions often lead to breakdowns in the communications process, so always give and get definitions.

Next, do not assume. Making assumptions invariably gets you into trouble. It's dangerous to assume that the person you're communicating with thinks or feels as you do at that moment. That person may have a very different frame of reference than you. Therefore, do not assume that you and the other person are talking about the same thing, or even that the words you are both using are automatically being understood. When you use more feedback and fewer assumptions, you'll be happier and more accurate in your interpersonal communications.

Another feedback guideline is to ask questions. Questions can be used to test for feedback. A good rule of thumb is: "When in doubt, check it out." One of the best ways to check it out is through the effective use of questioning that we discussed in a previous session.

It is important to speak the same language. My tip is to abstain from using words that can easily be misinterpreted or mistranslated, especially technical terms and company jargon. These terms, which are so familiar to *you,* may be totally foreign to the people you're talking to. Simplify your language and your technical terms so that everyone can understand you, even when you think the other person knows what the terms mean.

More good advice is to stay tuned in. You should constantly be on the lookout for those nonverbal signals that indicate the other person is becoming uncomfortable and losing interest in what you're saying. When this happens, change your approach and your message accordingly. I can't repeat this too often. Observe the other person, be sensitive to the feelings they're experiencing, and above all else, respond to those feelings appropriately.

Another especially important guideline is to give feedback on the behavior, not the person. This relates to the appropriate use of positive and negative strokes. When people do something especially well, give them positive feedback, and relate it specifically to the action or behavior they performed. And when they do something especially bad, give them negative feedback specifically about the action or behavior you would like corrected. Do not, under any circumstances, criticize the person personally because of an inappropriate action or behavior. This is not only degrading but also counterproductive. Many ineffective managers, when they learn that one of their employees has done something wrong, criticize that employee personally: They say things like "You're an idiot." or, "That was really stupid." Or, "You can't do anything right, can you?" These comments would be obvious inappropriate feedback. After a while, the employee starts believing these statements, and they become self-fulfilling prophecies. How can an employee improve performance on a particular task or behavior unless he or she knows specifically what behaviors or actions must be improved? So, direct your praise and punishment specifically to your employee's behavior and actions, not toward the employee personally.

Finally, let's talk about withholding feedback. Yes, there are times when it's best not to give feedback. In these situations, bite your tongue and restrain your body language and facial expressions. A few months ago, I was visiting a married couple. While waiting for the husband to finish getting dressed for an appointment, I was chatting with the wife in the dining room. All of a sudden, the husband came into the dining room in what appeared to be a huff. In a loud and harsh vocal intonation, he asked his wife, "Where did you get this shirt cleaned?!" While "asking" this assertion, he was shaking the collar of the shirt and seemed to be peering at his wife. The initial interpretation of this occurrence was that the husband was rather upset about the condition of his shirt. Most spouses would tend to act rather defensively, and some would even counterattack. His spouse was rather expert in withholding inappropriate feedback while at the same time asking for feedback. In a gentle voice with no disturbing body language, she simply told her husband: "I got it done at XYZ Cleaners. Why do you ask?" His reply almost floored me. He said it was the first time that any cleaners had done his shirt properly. He told his wife to take his shirts to that specific dry cleaner from now on. Clearly, there are times when it is best to withhold inappropriate feedback until you use effective feedback to clarify the intent of another person's message.

As you've seen, feedback can reduce interpersonal tension and create a sense of trust and credibility between you and the people you're communicating with, whether it's your co-workers, supervisors, employees, customers, or friends and family. It's as simple as confirming all uncertain verbal, vocal, and observable behaviors through feedback. This will help clarify messages, uncover important needs or problems, and make sure your message is being clearly received. Relationships can also be improved by using feedback because it lets the other person know what's going on in the relationship. Most of all, developing effective feedback skills will improve your part of the conversation. And of course, everyone wins when communications are clear and open.

Concentration and Focus

oncentration and Focus are the fourth qualities of the World's Greatest Communicators. You will learn there are both external and internal barriers that prevent us from being active listeners. To help you overcome those barriers, I will teach you easy techniques that will improve your ability to focus on other people as they speak.

One key issue is that the barriers to listening are not so easily identified. If you're trying to *see* something and there's a barrier in the way, it's usually pretty obvious, and you try to change your position to avoid whatever is blocking your sight. But sometimes we don't recognize when there's a noise barrier interfering with our hearing. I'm sure you've had the experience of sitting in a crowded restaurant, trying to talk with someone across the table when suddenly you notice that you're almost shouting to be heard and straining to hear the other person. It gets even more complicated if there's a lot of visual activity going on, people walking by and so on. And if you add music on top of that, the experience of trying to listen to someone becomes almost an Olympic event.

Let's assume you're prepared to give your best in the area of focus and concentration. That intention is fine, but there still may be barriers to listening actively. They include barriers that come from the environment, barriers that have to do with the speaker, barriers that result from the content of what's being said, and barriers that come from you, the listener.

Clearly, the most obvious **barrier in the environment** is competing noise such as music, traffic, a manufacturing process, TV, radio, or someone else talking loudly nearby.

Many people think they can concentrate on messages from two sources simultaneously; for instance, watching television and listening to someone in the room at the same time. Sorry, but your spouse is right. It's not possible to concentrate on two messages simultaneously at the same time. Although your *hearing* ability may be able to take in two different signals, your *listening* ability allows you to clearly process only one at a time.

One way to deal with a "message overlap" situation is to switch back and forth between the two messages, missing some of each and hearing some of each. Another way to handle the situation is to eliminate one of the noises, but that is not always possible. A third alternative is to focus selectively on only one of the two competing signals.

Selective listening means tuning out one set of signals and tuning into another. Your ear receives both signals, but your brain selects and focuses on the signal it wants to listen to. Imagine being in a restaurant where your table is touching the table of the couple next to you. You could tune into their conversation as easily as you tune into what the person across from you is saying. But you *choose* to listen to your tablemate and block out the conversation at the table next to you. That's selective listening and it takes effort.

There are some less obvious *barriers from the environment* beyond competing noise and voices. How about sitting in an uncomfortable chair, or in a room that's too hot, or too cold, or that has a bad odor? Each of these can be a distraction. Then there are physical disruptions such as telephone calls, visitors dropping in, or sirens going by—things you can't plan for. But again, you can minimize those kinds of distractions by adjusting your level of concentration and focus as necessary.

The second category of barriers arises from the **speaker**. These are "external" too, but they're not environmental. They're distractions that come from your perception of the speaker. These can include the way the speaker is dressed, whether he's clean-shaven, the smell of the perfume she's wearing, or whether their size or height is very different from yours. A friend once told me a story of how he was approached by a sales clerk who was very impressively dressed - expensive suit, shoes, tie, the works.

The sales clerk also had a fancy leather briefcase, and wrote with a very expensive pen. But my friend couldn't help but be distracted by the fact that the man was wearing white socks. He kept thinking: "What kind of person would go to all that trouble to look so sharp, and then wear white socks?" He obviously missed some of the sales clerk's message because he was distracted by his socks.

"Speaker-related" barriers can also include any mannerisms the speaker may have. Maybe she has a nervous twitch, or he stutters, or she keeps playing with the 12 rings on her fingers, or he says, "um" all the time. In addition, a speaker's facial expression can communicate anxiety, or anger, or flirtation. Each of those subtle messages can get in the way of really hearing what they're saying.

A third area where attributes of the speaker can get in the way of the message has to do with the person's regional or ethnic accent. I hope we're getting past it, but I know many people still think that certain accents connote intelligence or social standing more than others. Growing up, my strong Brooklyn accent likely made people think I was less intelligent than I actually was.

When you only have a voice to go by, do you find yourself reacting differently to the various accents? Does any one of them connote "highly educated" to you? Does any one of them connote a difference in social values from your own? Would you listen more intently to one of those voices? Would any of the accents cause you to listen less intently?

Unfortunately, many of us have developed biases for, or against, certain regional and ethnic accents. We make value judgments based on accent without knowing anything else about the person. And hearing one that we "think less of" can cause us to miss some of the person's message. Chances are, if you do react negatively to a particular accent, it would take more effort, more concentration on your part, to listen actively to someone speaking with that accent.

Depending on your own ethnic background and where you grew up, you may have favorable or unfavorable attitudes toward people with certain accents. Again, your ability to concentrate on someone speaking with a regional or ethnic accent will be challenged by your own biases.

If you are aware that your reactions to the accents do vary, then you've taken the first step. Awareness of your biases is necessary if you want to eliminate them.

A person's style of delivery can be a barrier for you too. The speaker could sound like he's pontificating as some great authority, or she could sound too sweet and little girl-like to be taken seriously as a vice-president. Some vocal "tones," like accents, can be pleasant and enhance the speaker's message for you, and some can turn you off. How fast, or how slowly, a person speaks is also an aspect of their style.

People who talk too fast risk the possibility that not everything they say will be heard, and worse, that they might be perceived as "a fast talker." The speed alone can create a negative attitude in the listener. Of course, the opposite problem—slow talkers—cannot only hinder their message, they can be downright painful.

Here's the reason. People can think at speeds as high as 400-500 words per minute, so with extremely slow speakers speaking at less than 100 words per minute, only 10 percent of your brain capacity is being used. It's impossible to shut off the other 90 percent, so your tendency will be to think of other things. Maintaining an active listening concentration with slow talkers takes a great deal of effort, but it can be done.

Another barrier that originates with the speaker has to do with the content of the message. Perhaps she's using words that aren't familiar to you and you don't want to indicate that you don't understand. Maybe what he's saying is full of buzzwords like "politically correct" or "environmentally conscious," and you're sure he doesn't know what he's talking about. Or maybe she's using some current lingo, such as New Age talk about "sharing space" or "finding your inner child," that may be hard to understand if you're not familiar with that school of thought.

There's also the situation where the speaker makes statements that are highly charged for you and your blood pressure starts to rise, especially in the areas of religion and politics. The challenge here is to exercise emotional control when the speaker's use of language gets in the way of your ability to listen effectively and objectively.

There are two quick tips I can give you to deal with these speaker-related barriers. One is to find out anything you can about the speaker in advance so you'll know what to expect. The second is to focus on the content of the message, not on the personality, the characteristics or the style of the speaker. In normal conversation, the message should take precedence.

Focusing on the content means simply learning what you can without forming judgments about the person. Easier said than done, I know. It will be a benchmark of your ability to listen actively when you can apply these techniques to content you really disagree with.

So far, we've talked about barriers to listening that arise from the environment, and from your perception of the speaker and his or her message. Next, we'll focus on barriers that come from inside you, the internal barriers. I'll give you some simple and effective techniques for overcoming most listening barriers.

There are two types of internal barriers to the listener. The first type is **physical**, and it's caused by any number of circumstances: you're tired, it's close to lunchtime, you've got a headache, you're feeling time constraints, you have to pick up your kid at baseball practice or from a dance lesson. Or maybe the person who is speaking is sitting too close to you, or too far away, and that is making you uncomfortable and you're finding it hard to concentrate.

The second type of internal barrier is **psychological**. This has to do with what your mind does as you listen. You daydream, or you're bored, or there's a little voice inside you that keeps discounting what you're hearing. Probably the most persistent psychological barrier is the tendency to let your mind wander away from the speaker. She may say something that triggers an image, or a past experience, or it triggers a warm glow or sadness or anger, and bingo—your mind is off and running in another direction.

Perhaps your past experiences don't jibe with what this person is telling you. Or the discussion isn't heading in the direction you hoped it would.

Another psychological barrier for a listener is the speaker's status relative to the listener.

For example, a person may require more effort and concentration to listen to a subordinate or colleague, even if they speak clearly, as compared to someone of superior status. Some of this may be due to the fact that in general we have more opportunity to consult with colleagues, than with the company president. But you lose out on important pieces of information if you turn off your concentration simply because of what you perceive the speaker's status to be, as well as how that person speaks.

An active listener knows how to eliminate the psychological barriers involving their attitude toward the status of the speaker.

A story from several years ago demonstrates "attitude toward the speaker," only this time the effect was reversed. Cathy had a son who worked on Bill Clinton's presidential campaign. The son was able to get his mother invited to a private gathering with President Clinton. As Cathy described it, she was in a large circle of people and Clinton was coming around to each person to say hello and have a brief chat. Cathy was a psychotherapist and had decided she'd use the opportunity to put in a plug for mental health care being a part of the overall health care reform package. When Bill Clinton got to her, she was able to say what she wanted to say, and to her surprise, the president engaged her in a five-minute conversation about what his reservations were on the subject. Cathy said later that she was so flustered that she didn't remember a thing he said. She had to ask the people around her what the president had said to her.

Here was a case where the high status of the speaker had created a major listening barrier. Cathy's story may be a bit unusual, but it's not hard to imagine that your ability to listen actively to a very important conversation might be compromised if you are overawed by the speaker.

One simple way to deal with all the barriers we've discussed—environmental, speaker-related, content-related, and listener-related—is to consider them as either within our control or not within our control. Some of the barriers, such as a noisy or uncomfortable environment, can at least be minimized, if not controlled.

You always want to create as comfortable an environment as possible, especially in terms of temperature and seating. That also means minimizing the competing sounds and the visual distractions

When you're meeting with someone in their environment and there are many distractions, you could recommend moving into another room with more privacy. More than likely, a person won't take offense if you point out a distraction they're not aware of when it's clearly in the service of your being able to hear them better.

The timing of the conversation has to be appropriate, too. For example, what's the best time to have a talk with a ten-year old child? Right after school? No. During prime-time TV? No, not even if you demand their attention. How about right at bedtime? Aha! Any ten-year old would be happy to have a conversation that extended the time before bed. Choosing the right timing with adults is a little trickier, but in general, seek out the times when they are most receptive to a conversation.

You probably do not have much control over distractions that come from the speaker, but you *can* do something about your perception of those distractions. And the things you can do are similar to what you need to do to take care of distractions that are content-related and that are internal to you. Let me give you four specific techniques that will help you concentrate and focus on the message whenever you encounter any of the listening barriers.

The first concentration technique is to *breathe deeply*. Yes, breathe deeply; it's as simple as that. Try it now.

Slowly breathe in, hold it, slowly breathe out, and relax. There are a lot of benefits to that simple act, but the main one I want to emphasize now is that *you* can't talk while you're breathing in. It prevents you from interrupting, or arguing with the speaker. And a deep breath helps you to focus on the present moment when you catch yourself drifting off and to refocus on the person speaking.

The second concentration technique is to *decide to listen*; that is, to make a conscious decision to listen to the other person. The philosopher Ralph Waldo Emerson once wrote: "Everyone in some way is my superior in that I can learn something from them." He did not only mean people he found interesting or likeable. His words hold for people you strongly disagree with or dislike as well.

The comedian Will Rogers is quoted as saying: "I never met a person I didn't like." Now do you think he ever ran into someone who rubbed him the wrong way? Of course he did. But his point was that he could find *one thing* he did like about the person, maybe one nugget, one gem of insight, one interesting fact. And you can too. The person may be boring, or may be saying things that you feel are completely irrelevant to your life. But, according to Rogers' philosophy, there is probably one thing you could learn from this person. Therefore you have to concentrate throughout the conversation because you never know when that one thing is going to show up.

The decision to listen is within your power. You just need to commit to it. When a distraction occurs, you can think: "I will listen to this person only." Now, most of us realize that when we're driving a car, a momentary distraction can lead to injury or even death. That's a compelling reason to concentrate. Usually there is not such a compelling reason when we are listening to somebody talk. But the driving example tells us we can concentrate when we decide to, for hours at a time, even when we're tired or uncomfortable.

A third technique for maintaining concentration allows you to capitalize on that speed differential I mentioned earlier: you can hear much faster than a person can speak. This technique is the art of *mental paraphrase*. That means you restate, translate, say in different words what the speaker is saying; only you keep it to yourself. Doing mental paraphrasing will keep you from daydreaming or shifting your mind to other topics. You'll keep your focus on the words of the other person and not on your own thoughts.

The fourth concentration technique is maintaining *eye contact*. It's called the hitchhiking theory—your ears follow your eyes. You're most likely to listen to what you're looking at. If you're looking at the face of the speaker, watching for facial expressions, seeing if the speaker is maintaining eye contact with you or is looking away, that will all help your concentration. Maintaining eye contact is a good technique, but be careful not to stare too long into the eyes of the other person. Looking directly into their eyes for too long sends a message that you want to either intimidate them or be intimate with them. Neither of those messages is helpful while you're trying to concentrate on the speaker.

You're probably beginning to realize how challenging these concentration skills can be. Let me remind you that the benefits are well worth it.

You will be able to communicate well in noisy environments, with people whose regional or ethnic accents used to create communication barriers for you. You will be able to focus on the content of a person's message and not have it be clouded by his or her personality. At the highest level of this skill, you will be able to focus on someone whose values totally contradict your own, and hopefully find some common ground in difficult situations. When you develop this ability to concentrate and focus, you're actually developing a key skill of a great communicator.

Strengthening and Improving Your Memory

Possessing a strong memory is the fifth quality of the World's Greatest Communicators. In this chapter, I will offer tips for strengthening and improving your memory. We'll take a look at how our understanding of memory has changed over the years, and how the value people assign to memory and the expectations they have about the power of memory have a huge impact on how well their memory works. This is a fascinating topic, so let's get started.

Memory has always been seen as an aspect of intelligence. In ancient Greece and Rome, for example, it was taken for granted that public figures would give speeches without notes. The very idea of reading a speech would have suggested that there was something seriously wrong. Of course, speaking without notes did not mean getting up there and just winging it. Speeches were written out and memorized and they could go on for several hours. It was taken for granted that a leader would have this kind of ability, just as it was taken for granted that they could read and write. However, memorizing speeches was just the beginning. In Greece, Alexander the Great knew the *Iliad* by heart. If you don't happen to have a copy of that epic poem handy, I can tell you that a modern paperback edition runs about 350 pages. So Alexander memorized it, as was expected, and so did many other aristocrats in ancient Greece.

Now we come to a very basic question about memory. Is a good memory either something you have or you don't have? Is it a gene you're given at birth, or is a weak memory a gene that you're missing? Or is memory something you can develop of your own free will? I happen to think the answer to that is very clear. Since virtually everybody with any education used to have amazing memory, it must be something that you can control. And that's exactly what the most recent work on memory is showing. Memory is a trait that you can develop and improve, just as you can get better at running or swimming. You can work at it and you can benefit from that work.

Making the most of your memory power is not something that happens by itself. From a practical standpoint, the process of memory has three parts.

- First, there's the formation of memory, which is called encoding.
- Then, there's the storage of memory.
- Finally, there's the recall of what has been encoded and stored.

Encoding is clearly very important, because if you do not form a memory to start with, there's no way you can call upon it later. For encoding to happen effectively, it has to be a conscious process. Like memory in general, it won't happen automatically. You have to make it happen—and in some situations that may require more focus and concentration than in the other two parts.

It's strange, isn't it? In the absence of injury or disease, the brain may record virtually everything that happens, but that doesn't mean it will be available to the conscious mind. In the same way, there are all kinds of television and radio signals in the air all the time, but unless you have your set turned on, you're not going to be able to watch the evening news. Attention, motivation, and interest are critical for encoding memories. Activating those three factors is like turning on your television set. They allow you clear access to what is out there in the world and to what is being recorded in your brain.

To see how this works, let's look at a classic situation for memory issues. You're at a cocktail party and you're introduced to a new person. You have a pleasant conversation, but suddenly it dawns on you that you've completely forgotten the name of your new friend. It's a very uncomfortable feeling and almost everybody has experienced it at one time or another. It also has some important lessons for improving your memory.

It's a natural tendency for people to divide their attention. When you're driving your car, you might want to listen to the radio. But do you remember what you hear on the radio? Do you remember what song or what commercial came just before the one you're hearing now? Frequently the answer is no, because divided attention undermines memory. Think about the cocktail party. Your attention is sure to be divided. There are many people talking, perhaps there's music, and maybe somewhere else you would rather be. When you are told someone's name, that information is coming into your consciousness along with plenty of other input. In some area of your brain, that name may be recorded for the rest of your life, but everything else is also being taken in. The information is absorbed in fragmentary form. Since your attention is not really focused on the name in an undivided way, that name is taken in as just another bit of static. It won't be easy to find it when you need it.

There are solutions to this problem, and they have importance beyond cocktail parties. Our attention is going to be divided much of the time just because of the world we live in. All kinds of input are coming into your consciousness—so you need to be fully aware of that. Attention has to be consciously given, or the memory is not going to be accessible.

Therefore, when you learn someone's name while in a setting with a lot going on, make a deliberate, conscious effort to focus on that name. But that's only the beginning. Most names are not very unique. People are named Jim or Jennifer or Tina or even Tony. Since it's easier to remember unusual information, you need to somehow make the usual names unique. Since memory is also strengthened by association, try associating the person's name with some other aspect of that person. If he's wearing a striped tie and his name is Jim, you might remember him as "Jungle Jim," because striped tigers live in the jungle. The more outlandish the connection is, the easier it will be to remember. So try it out.

I'm not the first one to introduce this technique. It is presented in many books on memory improvement. Though it is well known, very few people actually use it, which is too bad, because once you put the principles of uniqueness and association together, you can significantly increase your memory power. You can use these tools to remember almost any detail of your life that you might otherwise forget. But you have to make the conscious effort to use them. If your attention is divided, you have to be aware of that fact and you have to concentrate and focus. Otherwise, things are going to vanish. Short-term memory has a limited capacity. Information disappears fast unless you consciously prevent that from happening.

Next I will suggest some other tips you can use to improve short-term memory. As you read about them, say them out loud and see how well you can focus your attention. Really "listen," don't just "hear." In fact, practice doing this throughout the rest of this session. Since we're talking about attention as a tool for better memory, you can start using it right now.

First of all, when you take in some new information, try to take it in clearly and deeply as soon as possible. The first time you hear or see something is the best time to encode it in memory. Once information gets interference from more recent input, it becomes more difficult to access. Again, a clear illustration of this is the cocktail party. When you hear somebody's name for the first time, you use two very powerful memory tools we've mentioned before. The first is *intention*. In other words, make a conscious commitment to remembering what you hear. The second tool is *attention*, which is the way you put your commitment into action. When you intend to remember something, you can then use your attention to make sure you do in fact remember it. And remember: do this as soon as the new information presents itself.

Second, use the chunking process. That means breaking down larger pieces of information into smaller bits that are easier to remember. The seven-digit phone number is the best-known example of this. At some point in the past there was a genius who realized that phone numbers should take the form of a three-digit number followed by a four-digit number. It's amazing how much easier this is to recall. Even when you add another three-digit bit—which is the area code—the chunking method still seems to work. Why is this so effective? Everyone has limits on how much information they can recall, but those limits expand when the material is organized in chunks or bite-size form.

My first two tips focus mainly on remembering things you hear, so let's focus on remembering written material. Suppose there's an article you need to remember for an exam or a presentation. Most people will just start reading at the beginning and try to pay close attention until the end. As they proceed, many people will also highlight passages that seem important, but there are other more effective tools you can use. The first step to remembering written material, is to first read quickly through the whole thing. Some people call this skimming, and the real purpose is to get a general idea of the shape of the material. How is the article organized? What are the beginning, the middle, and the end? At this point, it's not about the details; it's just getting the lay of the land. You might just want to read the first sentence of each paragraph. For a ten-page article, this quick read shouldn't take more than a few minutes.

Now you are ready to read through the article a second time with a different intention. Instead of focusing on speed, you're now going to focus on content. So as you read, try to identify the key words that define the content of the material. Don't highlight passages. Focus on specific words that seem important, and then write those words in the margin beside the passages where they occur. If you're reading an article about economics, for instance, you may find yourself writing words like inflation or debt. Then, as you come to the end of each page, look at the key words you've written. Then, on a separate sheet of paper or in the margin at the top of the page, try to summarize the content of that page in a single sentence. But here's the key point—your summarizing sentence should be in the form of a *question*. By the time you are finished with this careful reading of the document, you should have one question that points you to the information on each page.

Now you are ready to look through the document again, for the third and final time. As you do so, find the words on each page that answer the question you've written at the top. This is a very solid approach to remembering written material. There's nothing very difficult about it. The main points are the quick initial read-through, and then summarizing the content of each page in the form of a question. And I want to emphasize again that highlighting is not an effective technique for remembering or studying a written text. So put away that yellow highlighter. All you really need is a pencil, a little time, and some focused attention.

Flash cards can be an effective memory aid, but mainly because of their convenience. You can carry them in your pocket and look at them whenever you have a free moment. Flash cards are especially good for very simple kinds of memorization, like learning state capitals or multiplication tables. One problem with flash cards is the temptation to cheat on yourself. You may start to remember things just because you've gotten used to the order of the cards. So shuffle the deck frequently.

Acronyms are a great way of remembering long lists of material. In fact, they may be the only really effective way to do this. All acronyms and other mnemonic techniques are based on the concept of elaborate encoding. The more meaningful and unique something is, the easier it is to remember. The brain isn't built to remember abstract symbols like numbers and playing cards, but if you can translate those symbols into a vivid image or phrase, even a meaningless series of numbers can be made memorable. The key is to develop a system that allows quick encoding and easy recall. Let's say you want to remember the colors of the spectrum, for example: red, orange, yellow, green, blue, indigo, violet. A common acronym for this is ROYGBIV, but a memorable sentence can be "Roosters only yell great big insults violently." What could be easier? In just a few seconds you have a perfectly workable sentence for remembering the colors of the spectrum. You can also use this tool for much longer strings of information. It is really a magical technique.

An interesting question about acronyms is whether they are somehow more attuned to the modern brain than other techniques that were used in the ancient world. Acronyms seem to work best for most people today, but the Greeks and the Romans were much more comfortable with creating a visual image in their minds to which they could attach information. One very popular technique involved imagining an amphitheater with rows and rows of seats. Each seat would be occupied by a certain piece of information. The student would close his eyes and actually see the amphitheater with the facts seated in row after row. These visualizations were called memory theaters, and some people developed them to an incredible degree. When you realize that an ancient amphitheater could hold fifty thousand people, you can imagine how far this can go.

The ancient world's memory techniques were so powerful they are still used today by memory experts or in memory competitions. Every year in London there is a contest to pick a world memory champion. The winners are always able to perform amazing feats of memory, but they do not seem to have extraordinary intelligence or unusual brain structures. The majority of these champions use the same memory strategy as the ancients. The material to be remembered is placed along an imaginary path. Then the information can be recalled by taking a visualized walk along the imaginary path. This technique was first described by a Greek poet in 477 BC and people are still using it effectively more than 2000 years later. The brains of certain individuals seem to have a hardwired gift for using spatial images to recall information. I suspect that this technique could be used by almost anyone who took the time to learn it. But for most people, acronyms seem to work better than visualized memory techniques and they are also a lot faster to use.

Ultimately, improving your memory is really a very personal matter. What works for someone else might not be the best method for you. Be aware of the moments when you want to use your brain at maximum effectiveness and find ways to reinforce that intention. One good way to do this is to use physical cues. By wearing a certain baseball hat, for example, you can send your mind a hint that now is a time to focus. If you often have material that you need to study or memorize, you might want to set aside a space where you perform this rather specialized activity. It can be a desk or a table in the corner of a room, but it should be set aside for this kind of work. There should not be overwhelming distractions, but a setting that is "too quiet" is not good either. Stephen King has certainly been a very productive novelist, and he likes to write with rock music blaring. For him, the music is more of an energy source than a distraction and silence would likely be much more intrusive on his concentration. Decide for yourself on the environment that works best for your own mental functioning.

Short sessions work best when you are trying to memorize difficult material. Break down the material into manageable bites, and create a schedule that will allow you to get the work done. Check your concentration and focus as you go. There will be times when you feel like doing more, and times when you want to do less.

Learning to remember is a very interesting process and it can be done very effectively. In a way, the reverse side of memory—forgetting—is more difficult to understand. Once something has been remembered, why doesn't it stay remembered? Or maybe it does stay remembered somewhere in the brain, but we just can't access it. Why do we lose memories, or seem to lose them? Why do we forget —and should we be happy or sad about it? Maybe forgetting isn't a problem at all. Do we really want to remember everything? There have been science fiction novels about characters who have unlimited conscious memory, and the plot outcome usually isn't good.

The truth of forgetting is that the brain may sometimes forget things because they are emotionally uncomfortable at an unconscious level—but on other occasions remembered material may just be covered up by newer input. In this way, forgetting may be one area of brain function that actually is like a computer. On some internet servers, if you don't open an email within a certain period of time, it begins to move lower down the list of received messages.

To extend the metaphor a little further, there is usually also a button on the email labeled "keep as new." Our brains work similarly. If you want to prevent something from being forgotten, you need to focus on it, which tells your brain to label it "keep as new." If you don't take this conscious action, the natural process of giving priority to new information will take place and the old information may be forgotten.

The more you work to strengthen and improve your memory, the more your skill as a great communicator will also increase.

Conflict
Resolution

The sixth quality of the World's Greatest Communicators is Conflict Resolution. In this chapter we will identify sources of conflict and how to encourage healthy disagreement without spiraling down into negative conflict. We will discuss tools to help you resolve conflict once it's begun.

It is important to acquire conflict resolution skills because it would be a mistake to attempt to completely erase disagreement from our lives, even if we could. People naturally disagree about what to do and how and when to do it. That interaction of ideas and opinions sparks new ideas and leads to better solutions and action plans. However, when differences of opinion are accompanied by too much emotional commitment to one point of view versus another, the resulting conflict can be damaging.

Conflict arises from the clash of perceptions, goals, or values. You see it your way, he sees it his way, and tension ignites. However, conflict can lead to productive growth if it is properly managed and resolved. The key element affecting conflict is communication: it is both the cause and the remedy. On the remedy side, it is open communication that can prevent, manage, and resolve disagreement.

Because of its many causes, there is no way to avoid conflict in today's rapidly changing environment. But conflict can be managed and the first step is to understand it.

Conflict can occur at several levels: between individuals, between groups, and between organizations, and it typically proceeds through four stages, as identified by theorist Louis Pondy.

Phase one is the **Latent Phase**. This is where there is potential for conflict when two or more parties must cooperate in order to achieve a desired objective.

Phase two is the **Perceived_Phase**. This is the point when members are becoming more aware of a problem and tension begins, even if they are not sure where it comes from.

Phase three is the **Felt Phase**, where the parties begin to focus in on differences of opinion and interests, which sharpens perceived conflict.

Phase four is the **Manifest Phase**. At this point, the outward display of conflict occurs when the opposing parties plan and follow through with acts to frustrate one another.

As conflict proceeds through these stages, resolution becomes more difficult. The *ideal* is to recognize conflict early and work for a resolution that is a win for each party.

Let's now look at several **conflict management** options. Each strategy has advantages and disadvantages. One strategy might work better for a particular situation than another.

We'll start with **Avoidance**. This is an instinctive, simple response to conflict. By not confronting the problem, neither party is labeled winner or loser. However, this strategy rarely works, because it does nothing to make the conflict go away. On the other hand, if the problem is inconsequential, this can be an appropriate option as in the example of a manager who avoids getting involved with a minor employee dispute.

Another option is **Accommodation**, which happens when someone "gives in" without actually working through the conflict. For example, a supervisor wants an employee to do something a new way. The employee says, "Oh, all right—but I really think it's better my way." The employee has accommodated the supervisor but there is no real resolution since the base issues are left unresolved.

Although accommodation includes cooperative effort, it still requires sacrifice, turning conflict into a win-lose situation, which is often merely a temporary fix. This exploitation of cooperative elements is, however, beneficial when the accommodating party feels little personal involvement with the issue, or has little to lose by giving in to the other person. Accommodation may also ensure positive future relations.

Domination is a win-lose strategy that involves a struggle for power and domination over another party. The most powerful party, in some cases the manager, or a parent or teacher, imposes a solution. Domination does have its benefits: it resolves conflicts quickly and it is effective when the parties recognize and accept the power relationship.

If overused, this strategy can create resentment among involved parties since goals may be reached at another's expense. Consistent "losers" might feel that their needs will never be met and they begin to withdraw from the conflict altogether. Like Accommodation, Domination is generally only a temporary solution because it too fails to treat the root of the conflict.

Negotiation can be a suitable strategy for resolving conflicts because it is a compromising effort that involves moderate levels of cooperation and assertiveness. It does, however, have its own inherent pitfalls. With this strategy, both sides state their positions and try to reach an acceptable compromise. Most negotiations attempt to minimize losses while maximizing gains or creating a situation where everyone partially wins and partially loses. In salary negotiations, for example, every dollar the employee "wins," the company "loses." This compromising effort can lead to a situation where no one is completely satisfied. In sensitive negotiations, it is easy for the parties to tip the scale into a more assertive mode and wind up in a standoff, which is a very serious pitfall.

The art of **Collaboration** can be very effective in conflict resolution, although it requires a high level of cooperation and assertiveness. It can be effective because rather than depending on negotiation or compromise, collaboration relies on creative problem solving to identify solutions that will meet the needs of all the parties. Rather than just negotiating salary, the employee and the supervisor might discuss at length the employee's goals and objectives and how they fit in with the organization's goals and objectives. Collaboration takes time and effort, but it addresses the underlying issues of the situation, which makes it a generally long-lasting and productive conflict resolution strategy.

Obviously, if it is important to resolve a conflict in a way that enhances the relationships involved, collaboration is far more effective than avoidance or the other strategies of conflict resolution. Let's dig a little deeper into this strategy and look at the four basic components of collaboration, which are:

- understanding and respecting the goals and objectives of each of the parties
- assertiveness
- creative problem solving
- confrontation

Collaboration assumes equality in the standings of the parties, which is why understanding and respecting are key components. Even if there are differences in the power or status of one or more of the parties, in this conflict resolution strategy, the goals and objectives of each person are accepted to be equal. Of course, after presenting each person's goals and objectives, they may need to be ranked and evaluated logically, but it's done with the participation of all of the parties. Each member of the group tries to stay focused on the organization's goals rather than on individual objectives.

For a collaboration to succeed everyone must feel safe in expressing their ideas and opinions; in other words, they need to have a certain degree of assertiveness. Each position needs to be presented as powerfully as possible. People often confuse assertiveness with aggression. Here's the difference: aggression is assertiveness without regard for the needs of the other person. Assertiveness says: "Here's my position; what's yours?" Aggression is: "Here's my position; take it or leave it."

The third component of collaboration is creative problem solving. This skill can help define a solution that results in a win for each person. Those who are proficient in this area focus on the problem rather than on specific solutions. They spend time identifying as many potential solutions as possible before proceeding with evaluation. They also avoid dwelling on the history of the problem, which often involves placing blame.

Confrontation is the fourth component of collaboration, which is a specific communication strategy. It is a way to change behavior through constructive feedback. During an emotionally charged conflict resolution session, it is often necessary to use confrontation to break through a communication barrier. Let's look at an example. Two co-workers have competing priorities, which has created conflict. Co-worker #2 consistently is late delivering necessary information to Co-worker #1.

Co-worker #1 may decide to confront Co-worker #2 by explaining to him the impact his behavior is having on the organization. Confrontation can be a very effective strategy, but it has to be done skillfully or it can escalate the conflict. Because of its potential to resolve conflicts, confrontation merits a deeper examination. Let's walk through a model for handling different levels of conflict through confrontation.

First of all, there are levels of confrontation: at the beginning of the continuum, there may be a simple misunderstanding or a sense by one party that the other is not hearing him. At the other end of the continuum, the conflict may be so severe it is jeopardizing the goals of the organization. At the beginning of the continuum, we're trying to achieve understanding, and at the other end, we're demanding a change in behavior. As you move along the continuum, there are different confrontation strategies that can be used to resolve the conflict. They are progressive, so as the conflict moves from merely being a matter of achieving understanding to a greater need for behavior change, the confrontation can incorporate each of the following strategies.

We begin with **Reflection**. In this stage, you demonstrate your sincere desire to understand the person's feelings and needs. You are gathering data and building rapport with the person. By reflecting the feelings you hear the person expressing, you give him a chance to correct your impression and elaborate on your comment. Here's the form these statements generally take: "I understand that you feel or think 'blank,' because of 'blank.'" Here's an example: "I understand that you feel unappreciated, because you are not invited to the weekly staff meetings."

The next level of strategies uses what is called an **I-statement**. With this type of statement, you reveal *your* feelings, asserting your own needs and objectives in a non-judgmental fashion. You want the other person to understand your feelings and reasons. These statements follow this general form: "I feel a certain way when you do a certain thing *because* 'blank.'" An example would be "I feel angry when you ignore the safety rules *because* you and others might get hurt."

The **Diplomatic Disagreement** stage is where you are trying to achieve understanding in a tactful gentle manner. You want the person to know you value the relationship, but you also want the other person to understand your reasoning while you try to understand his. The format for this stage includes refection and an I-statement. For example, "I understand that you think we need a new computer. I appreciate your position and realize you think it will improve our productivity, but I believe we should wait because a new model is about to be released."

Another stage is **Gentle Confrontation**, where you are actually trying to cause a change in behavior and build the relationship at the same time. You want to suggest the change in a tactful, somewhat tentative fashion. The format includes reflection, an indication that the other person is valued, an I-statement, and an indication of consequences. It would go like this: First the reflection:

"You think the accounting department should pay our vendors immediately." Then, valuing the person: "I appreciate your position and understand it helps you negotiate better prices." Next, an I-statement: "However, I feel frustrated because I'm trying to manage our cash flow as well as our profits." And finally, an indication of consequences: "If you continue to pressure the accounting department, it will make it much more difficult for me to manage the cash flow and investments. That could result in vendors going unpaid and a reduction in profits that could impact our profit sharing."

Moving up a level is **Firm Confrontation**. This is where you are trying to clear up disagreements and cause a definite change in behavior, which is your primary objective. The format of this confrontation is the same as the Gentle Confrontation example, with the *added* statement: "In the future I would appreciate it if you would come to me for any special early payment requests."

Throughout the entire confrontation process, there are three basic guidelines that will help make the process more productive.

The first is **Timing**. You need to ask, "Is the person ready to listen?" If you are trying to tell someone why showing up late for work every day isn't in his best interests, doing it right after he checks in, is probably not a good time. He's probably feeling defensive. Wait until you have something positive to say about his performance. Then, you can tell him how his tardiness is affecting the overall perception of his commitment and performance.

Next guideline is to **Focus** on current specifics. Talk about behavior that is happening today, not something that happened last week or last month.

The third guideline is to **State Your Feelings**. When you tell someone how you feel, you are keeping the conversation open, rather than focusing it only on the other person. In the case of the tardy employee, I'd say "When you come to meetings late, I feel really angry because the rest of us have to wait for you before we can start on the project."

Confrontation is a powerful conflict resolution strategy that requires a great deal of skill and practice. It is also important to remember that people only change when it is in their best interest to do so. You cannot make another person change, no matter how persuasive your argument, but you can increase his motivation to do so by appealing to his self-interest.

If, for example, you are irritated by a coworker's behavior, you can focus less on how he affects you and more on how your reaction affects him. In this case, you might let this coworker know that you feel less inclined to work with him on his project because of his particular behavior.

It is important to remember that people are often afraid to be confrontational and assertive because they are unsure of the reaction they will get. Most of us try to avoid confrontations that might create anger, defensiveness, or rejection. You can avoid this reaction and still be assertive, through the sensitivity with which you express your concerns. The confrontation continuum I discussed gives you a series of strategies to help you assert yourself in a way that reduces rather than accelerates conflict. One reason these strategies produce this result is that they help us achieve understanding or a change in behavior without destroying the other person's morale.

So far, I have presented tips and strategies for what you *should* do. But sometimes, it's not enough to know only what we *should* do. We also need to recognize those things that we *should not* do. In a conflict, emotions may be extremely sensitive and we may offend without intending to. Here are some actions to avoid because they generally escalate a conflict rather than resolve it.

Don't Minimize. Sometimes we don't recognize the seriousness of an action or perception, and we make light of it through humor or sarcasm. When this happens the other person feels unvalued or belittled. Often the person takes your minimization as a personal attack. When someone brings a problem to our attention, the first thing we need to do is acknowledge it. Consider the following responses to a statement and see which one you think is more effective.

- An engineer says, "I'm afraid the O-ring might fail at low temperatures."
  - Manager 1 replies, "That's not your problem. Worry about how we're going to meet our next deadline."
  - Manager 2 says, "I appreciate your concern, what makes you think that?"

Another common mistake is to assign **Blame**. While blame can often be attached to the last person who touched a situation, many problems are too complex to be caused totally by one person or one factor. The focus should be on preventing future problems rather than placing blame. Again, consider these two responses by managers:

- A salesperson says, "We didn't get the Smith account."
    - Manager 1 implies blame by asking, "What did you do wrong?"
    - Manager 2 is more future minded by asking, "What could we have done better?"

Unloading is another thing to avoid. When people have worked together for a long time, there are often numerous small grievances that have gone unmentioned. When a larger problem sparks a conflict, the temptation to unload that past baggage is often overwhelming. While it might make the person who is unloading feel better, it's certainly not a productive conflict resolution strategy. So when an employee arrives at work late, it would be unloading if a manager said, "Not only are you late today, but last week there was an addition error in the report you submitted and you never have turned in the Murphy proposal that was due over a month ago." A better response would be "Is everything ok? I know you were only a few minutes late, but you normally seem so committed, and recently you seemed to be distracted. Is there anything I can do?"

Low Blows are definitely to be avoided. As we work with people, we begin to understand their sensitivities. Hitting one of those emotionally touchy areas can escalate a conflict out of control and make it very difficult to regain the lost ground. If an employee misses a meeting, no one will gain points by saying "No wonder you were fired from your last job. Obviously you're incapable of managing your time."

Also avoid **Manipulation**, where a person uses personal charm or approval to get someone to do something without regard to the other person's needs or objectives. This also includes withholding approval or rewards in order to get the desired action. An example would be a manager saying "If you'll work overtime tonight, I'll remember it when review time comes up." It's better to give the reason why the overtime is needed.

The use of **Force**, as in the "I don't care what you want, do it my way, now!" approach should also be avoided. Of course, it works if all you want is to get an immediate action. And, if it's only used on extremely rare occasions, it is an effective way to get something done immediately. However, it is demoralizing to the other person because it fails to acknowledge their worth or their ideas.

Now I'm going to share five basic behaviors that will help you resolve conflict in almost any situation you encounter. By using them, you can benefit from positive disagreement without having them escalate into out-of-control personality conflicts that damage the morale and productivity of the organization. Here they are:

Always project an attitude of **Openness**. State your feelings and thoughts openly and honestly without trying to hide the real object of your disagreement. Use I-statements and talk about how you feel and what you want. Focus on current specifics and on identifying the problem.

Listen with **Empathy.** Try to understand and feel what the other person is feeling, and to see the situation from their point of view. This includes demonstrating your understanding and validating the other person's feelings. Make comments such as

- "I appreciate how you feel."
- "I understand your feelings."
- "I'm sorry I made you feel that way."

Let the other person know you are sincere in understanding their views.

Demonstrate **Supportiveness**. Describe the behaviors you have difficulty with rather than evaluating them, and express your concern for and support of the other person. You want the person to know your intention to find a solution that benefits both of you. State your position tentatively, with a willingness to change your opinion if appropriate reasons are given. You need to be willing to support the other person's position if it makes sense to do so.

Have an attitude of **Positiveness** by trying to identify areas of agreements and then emphasize them. Look at the conflict as a way to better understand the entire situation and to possibly find a new and better solution. Be positive about the other person and your relationship, expressing your commitment to finding a resolution that works for everyone.

The fifth basic behavior that will help you resolve conflict is to *treat the other person and their ideas and opinions as* **equal**. This means giving the person the time and space to completely express their ideas. Then, evaluate all ideas and positions logically and without regard to ownership.

As I stated when I began, conflicts offer many benefits if we can resolve them productively. For one, as people are forced to work through a problem to a solution, they need to understand the point of view of others. In addition, successful resolution of small conflicts can diffuse the possibility of more serious conflicts and result in better working relationships.

Sometimes it's only through the conflict resolution process that we identify and highlight key issues that were rumbling under the surface and needed a healthy debate to become apparent. How well we manage conflict can be a critical skill in quality communications.

Presentation Power

This chapter will provide you with effective tips for increasing your Presentation Power, which is the seventh Quality of the World's Greatest Communicators.

Just how important is this skill? A study conducted by AT&T and Stanford University revealed that the top predictor of success and upward mobility, professionally, is how much you enjoy public speaking and how effective you are at it. Unfortunately, the number one fear of most adults—even above death—is speaking in public.

To help you increase your skills in this area, we will examine these three areas: overcoming stage fright, preparing for a successful presentation, and using visuals effectively.

Almost every speaker, actor, musician, and performer experiences stage fright, that feeling of sweaty palms, jelly knees and a stomach filled with butterflies. While the fear never goes away entirely, you can learn to manage it.

First, you must understand that stage fright is a very normal reaction, and it can be overcome if you're ready to approach it with the right attitude. The way you look at yourself, the audience, the subject, preparation and delivery, and the anxiety itself has a direct impact on how you will feel when you walk toward the podium.

An important step is to remember that stage fright is normal and to be open about it. Sometimes just admitting you're feeling anxiety helps relieve it. You should also remember that you are the expert, and that the person who asked you to speak believes you have something of value to share. The people attending the meeting also believe they will receive information of value. Concentrating on them and their needs will help you forget about your own self-consciousness.

Here are nine additional tips for overcoming stage fright:

1. Know your material well. Be the expert.
2. Practice your presentation. Do a pilot test, and if possible, videotape yourself.
3. Get the audience to participate.
4. Establish rapport by using names and eye contact.
5. When possible, check the facilities in advance.
6. Research your audience. Get acquainted with at least one person in the audience.
7. Relax. Breathe deeply and visualize yourself successfully presenting your message to the audience.
8. Use visuals, both to prompt you and to make a visual impact on the audience.

9. And finally, use your own style. Don't imitate someone else.

As an audience member we have all experienced presentations, ranging from the dynamic, mesmerizing speaker, to the person who reads his notes in a never-ending drone. What makes one presentation better than the next? The following characteristics of an effective speaker should answer that question:

- He or she understands the needs of the audience and attempts to meet those needs as effectively as possible.
- An effective speaker is the expert on the subject and has a breadth of knowledge in other areas.
- An effective speaker is constantly growing and improving her understanding in her areas of expertise and the ability to present the material effectively.

Here are some more characteristics. The effective speaker:

- Is enthusiastic about the subject and sincere about conveying the message.
- Has a pleasing voice and appearance.
- Uses examples, illustrations, analogies and stories to make information more interesting and exciting.
- Paces the program to keep it lively and interesting, using an appropriate level of humor and drama.
- Makes information as practical as possible, telling people "how" to use the information.

While it may not be possible to possess all these charac-teristics completely, the following guidelines will help you incorporate these traits.

The success of your public speaking is determined primarily by the time you spend preparing before you step in front of your audience. A good presentation requires careful planning and a lack of planning is always apparent. Sure clues are speeches that are too long, too detailed, confusing, vague, boring, or off-track.

The often-overlooked first and most critical step in preparation is to understand the "what" and the "why" of your presentation, in other words, its purpose. This is the broad general outcome you want the presentation to achieve. Here are three questions you can ask yourself to clarify the objective of your presentation:

- Why am I giving this presentation?
- What do I want the audience to know or do at the end of the presentation?
- How do I want the audience to feel?

It helps that we understand the four different types of presentations: **sales, exploratory, instructional,** *and* **oral report.** These four differ primarily in the amount of detail presented and the level of persuasiveness required to meet the objective of the presentation. Let's look at each one.

You would use the **sales presentation** to sell an idea or suggestion to clients, upper management, co-workers, or employees. You may also use the sales presentation to persuade an audience to take a particular action or adopt a belief. This type of presentation uses several persuasive skills and seldom requires extensive detail.

The **explanatory presentation** is best used to give an overall perspective, or identify new developments. It should rarely involve heavy detail, but should offer the audience new or renewed information and understanding. It does not require extensive persuasive efforts.

When you want to teach others how to use something, such as a new procedure or a piece of hardware, you use the **instructional presentation**. There is usually more audience participation and involvement with this presentation format. It generally involves extensive detail and is a persuasive presentation because your goal is to convince your audience to use a new technique or to adopt a new method of doing something.

Oral reports bring the audience up to date on something they are already familiar with. These generally focus on facts, figures, and other details and involve little persuasive efforts.

After you have a statement of purpose, and understand the type of presentation you will be giving, you need to take into account the particular **audience** you have in mind. You will want to mold your presentation to fit the specific characteristics of that audience. The more time you devote to analyzing your audience beforehand, the less you will have to do "on the spot."

There are a number of ways you can get information in advance about your audience. You can ask the presentation host about the general demographics such as age, sex, professional level, specific interests and needs. You could also ask what the group has responded well to in the past and what presentation styles were well received.

You can talk to members of the audience. If possible, arrive early enough to survey one or more members of the audience to find out what they expect and what they would like to hear.

Talking to other speakers is also an excellent way to obtain information, especially if you know some who have addressed the same group. You can ask them what worked and what they would do differently with the group.

Here are some questions you should always ask yourself to help analyze the needs of each audience you will address.

- Why should they listen to you?
- How does what you say affect them?
- What's in it for them to listen to you?
- Why is it important for the audience to hear what you have to say?

The next step in the preparation process is determining the **specific objectives** of your presentation. What is the desired change in a participant at the end of the session? You should describe your objective from the audience's point of view, making it is as specific as possible. To make your presentation truly effective, you need to make your objective realistic. Ask yourself these questions:

- Can you accomplish your objective in both the available preparation time and presentation time?
- Does your audience have the necessary knowledge and background to achieve your desired results?

- Do the audience members have the authority to make the decisions you may want them to make?
- Are resources available for you to accomplish your ideas?
- Do key individuals stand in the way of your goals?

Once you know your audience and are clear about your objectives, you are ready to start organizing your presentation. The first step is to find your **focus**. This is the Big Idea of your material—the power punch—the one thing you want your audience to walk away with.

How well you translate your material—your message—into benefits for the audience will determine its effectiveness. Structure your presentation so that it supports your one Big Idea. Of course, your message will contain more than one idea but they should all reinforce the primary focus.

One way to make sure you are clear on your focus is to develop a basic outline of your presentation. Begin by listing no more than five independent ideas the audience must understand for the objectives to be accomplished. Then, outline your plan in a way that the necessary detail and persuasive material will allow your audience to understand those points. This gives you a rough outline of the content of your message.

In any presentation, there are three major sections: the introduction, main body, and conclusion. Your first step is to get the audience's attention and convince them to listen to you. This happens in the introduction, and sadly, this is where many beginning speakers lose their audience. You need to grab them with something vitally interesting to them. Give them an interesting story or example that ties into your focus. Use a strong, meaningful quotation or a startling statistic. A speaker who begins by saying, "According to statistics, by this time next year, one person in this room will be dead" would pique my interest about his message. Or another speaker who states "According to experts, 50% of all speakers make up their statistics" would give me a chuckle and begin to draw me into the presentation.

Never apologize! This is one thing you should never do, and you'd be surprised how many novice speakers do this. Even if the airline lost your bag and you're in yesterday's clothes or if you're a last minute substitute for the best speaker in the country or if you have the flu and a 101 degree temperature! Don't mention it. The minute you apologize, your ability to influence your audience is decreased. You want to do everything you can to make sure none of those negatives happen, but if they do, go on. Start your speech with power. Make your audience think they're going to be informed, entertained or enlightened. Don't let them think they're getting inferior goods, leftovers or anything except your best.

It's important to write out your introduction completely, word-for-word. In addition, it should prepare the audience for the main points of the presentation to come. This part of your presentation is too important to leave to chance, hoping you have the right words when you get there. It also acts as a security blanket. If you can get through those first few minutes, the butterflies will settle down and the rest of the presentation will flow more easily. As a rule of thumb, the introduction should take 5 to15 percent of the allowed speaking time.

Here are the main elements that are generally included in an introduction.

- Begin your talk with a bang: an attention-getter. An anecdote or humor can ease and relax both the audience and you, but only use what is appropriate and relevant. If you're presenting an action plan to deal with nuclear war, a humorous opening is probably not be appropriate
- Next, involve the audience by letting them know that your information is relevant to their needs.
- Increase your credibility by relating something about your background and expertise. This makes your audience more receptive.
- It's a good idea to present your agenda, keeping in mind the familiar phrase: "Tell them what you are going to tell them, tell them, and then tell them what you just told them."
- Let the audience know what you expect of them. At the beginning of your presentation, tell listeners about the Q&A session at the end, or the ensuing reception, or the cards you want them to fill out before they leave.

In many presentations to smaller groups, it might be helpful to do an opening ice-breaking exercise. This sets an emotional climate for the presentation. It also gets people talking and involved with the focus of your message. The most common icebreaker is having people introduce themselves and explain their reason for attending the presentation. Simple games that are fun and get people involved are an excellent way to get a session started.

Here are the three most important criteria for a good icebreaker:

- They should be short—about five to ten minutes.
- They should be appropriate—that is, they should have something to do with the topic.
- They should be participative—something that each person can, and wants to get involved in.

Now that you've gotten the audience's attention, you need to deliver what you promised in the shortest, most interesting way possible. James Roosevelt, son of FDR once said, "My father gave me this advice on speech making: 'Be sincere. Be brief. Be seated.'"

Remember that the purpose of your presentation is not to present all you know about a subject. It is to present what your audience needs to know in a way that meets your personal objectives as well as theirs.

Two very important things to keep in mind as you structure your message are the attention cycle of your audience and pacing.

It can be discouraging to look into the audience only to note the number of persons with drooping eyelids and slumping bodies. Obviously, their attention span has fizzled. There are ways you can regain their interest. First, you have to understand the basics of the attention cycle.

Studies have shown that material at the beginning and the end of a presentation will be remembered more than what is in the middle. Our attention span only lasts for a short time and then it tapers off. When we sense the end of a message, we pull our attention back in time to catch the last material. Fluctuation of the attention cycle is one of the main reasons we put such emphasis on the introduction and conclusion.

But how do we hold people's attention during the main body of our message? Simply, we create several mini-cycles with beginnings, middles, and ends instead of having one big cycle that lasts through the entire presentation. This is called "pacing." The late, great speaker, Bill Gove, called it vignettes.

You should plan a change-of-pace approximately every 7 to 8 minutes so you can break up your talk into mini-cycles and keep attention riveted. You can do this by including appropriate humor, stories, exercises requiring people to move their bodies—even if it's just raising their hands—or calls for a verbal response. Make these change-of-pace exercises as physical as possible if your presentation occurs after lunch when much of our energy is diverted to our digestive system.

In addition to changing your pace frequently, here are four techniques you can use to help your listeners remember more of your message.

- **Repetition:** Let the beginning of your presentation whet their appetites for the main message and let the wrap-up reinforce the main points of the message and include a call for action. Your main ideas should be stated more than once, using different words to keep the presentation from being redundant or boring.

- **Association and connection:** When you use stories and analogies that connect your ideas to something your listeners already understand, it helps them grasp and remember your message.

- **Intensity:** Your tone of voice can reflect the passion you have about your message. You can also convey the emotional content of your message by telling gripping, relevant stories, and by relating the message to the lives and values of those in your audience.

- **Involvement:** Your presentation should appeal to as many senses as possible, since people have different methods of processing information. Some are visual learners, some auditory, and some emotional. Use visuals, hand gestures, and sound effects—anything that gets the audience involved with the message.

These techniques keep attention at a high level and help people remember your message. Of course, there are other techniques you can use to sharpen your presentation. You should consider using examples because of the quick and powerful way they can transmit your message.

When used sparingly and presented simply, statistics can add drama and credibility to your message. Comparisons can help your audience evaluate different options quickly and logically. And including testimonies, such as personal stories or tributes of a credible person can make your message more believable.

Now that we have moved through the opening and the main body of the presentation, it is time to consider the conclusion. Many speakers have a dynamite opening and a powerful, interesting message, only to drop the ball at the end. You need a strong wrap-up because it serves an important role for the audience. This is where you sum-up and stress the main ideas you want the audience to remember and where you call for and encourage appropriate action.

Your conclusion should repeat your main ideas. This is not the time to introduce a new point, because you can't expect an audience to remember a point they've only heard once. You can signal the wind-up of your presentation with a phrase such as: "Let's review the main points we've covered." By reviewing, you give the audience a chance to reaffirm that they know and understand the main message covered during the session. Your conclusion should be strong, succinct, and persuasive. Many speakers consider this section almost as important as the introduction and they write it out word-for-word.

You know your audience. You know your material. You have written a dynamite speech. The last step is to practice delivering it. These guidelines can help:

- I recommend that you rehearse out loud. You do this in order to check your timing since you read out loud slower than you read in your mind, and to make sure your presentation flows and sounds the way you want it to.

- Rehearse at least four or five times. You should feel comfortable explaining all your ideas. But don't try to memorize your speech or you may end up sounding stale, as if you are reciting or reading.
- When possible, it is beneficial to rehearse in the actual location of the presentation. It is certainly better to work out the technicalities of any visuals and positioning during a rehearsal as opposed to the day of your presentation.
- Time yourself during rehearsal. Do this during your last few rehearsals so you can make sure you stay within the amount of time allotted for your presentation.
- Rehearse in front of people. You can get used to public speaking by rehearsing with family or friends. To help make sure your message is clear, ask them to explain what they heard. Ask them if your visuals are effective and if they make your message more understandable. And of course, ask them what you can do better.

Once you've rehearsed your presentation and feel comfortable with the material, visualize yourself presenting it.

As I stated at the beginning of this great communication quality, your ability to speak in front of groups is one of the most important professional skills you can develop. This is because the ability to make public presentations is said to be the number one predictor of the level of professional success. The tips and guidelines I've presented here will go a long way in helping you develop that skill. But to truly become a great communicator, you have to practice it in front of real, live audiences. Force yourself to find opportunities to speak. Volunteer at your professional organizations, civic clubs, or church. You might even consider joining Toastmasters where you benefit from a weekly speaking experience in a supportive, educational environment. With practice, you can become a great presenter and great communicator.

Communication Adaptability

The eighth quality of the World's Greatest Communicators is Communication Adaptability, which is your willingness and ability to adjust your communication based on the particular needs of the situation or relationship at a particular time. It is something applied more to yourself (to your patterns, attitudes and habits) than to others.

For any situation, the strategic adjustments that need to be made will vary. The decision to employ specific adaptability techniques is made on a case-by-case basis: you can choose to be adaptable with one person, and not so with others. You can choose to be quite adaptable with one person today and less adaptable with that same individual tomorrow. Adaptability concerns the way you manage your own behaviors. It means adjusting your own behavior to make other people feel more at ease with you and the situation.

Adaptability does not mean "imitation" of the other person's communication style. It does mean adjusting your communication style in the direction of the other person's preference, while maintaining your own identity.

Adaptability is important to all successful relationships. Effectively adaptable people meet other people's needs in addition to their own. Through practice, they are able to achieve a balance—strategically managing their adaptability by recognizing when a modest compromise is appropriate, or, when the nature of the situation calls for them to totally adapt to the other person's style, they do so. Adaptable people know how to negotiate relationships in a way that allows everyone to win. They are tactful, reasonable, understanding, and nonjudgmental.

Your adaptability level influences how others judge their relationship with you. Raise your adaptability level and trust and credibility go up; lower your adaptability level and trust and credibility go down. Adaptability enables you to interact more productively with difficult people and helps you to avoid or manage tense situations. With adaptability, you can communicate with other people the way *they* want and need to be communicated with. It is practicing the *Platinum Rule* during interpersonal communications rather than the *Golden Rule* which states: "Do unto others as you would have them do unto you." The *Golden Rule* implies the basic assumption that other people would like to be treated the way that *you* would like to be treated. The *Platinum*

Rule accommodates the feelings of others. "Treat others the way *they* want to be treated." The focus of relationship shifts from "this is what I want, so I'll give everyone the same thing" to "let me first understand what they want and then I'll give it to them."

The concept of adaptability, as developed by Dr. Michael O'Connor, my co-author of our *People Smart* books, is a two-part process. It combines **flexibility** with **versatility.** Flexibility is your *willingness* to adapt. It is your attitude. Versatility is your *ability* to adapt. It is your aptitude.

When you have *both* flexibility and versatility, you display specific characteristics. In fact, formal research studies have identified 10 attributes of people who are highly adaptable. Those who have lower adaptability also display 10 distinct characteristics. Of course, none of us is totally adaptable, or totally non- adaptable, which is why it is so important to know both the 10 characteristics you can adopt to increase your communication adaptability and the 10 that can undermine your ability to adapt.

So let's examine these characteristics, beginning with the five positive and five negative qualities of flexibility. **High flexibility** is characterized by these five attributes:

- Confidence
- Tolerance
- Empathy
- Positiveness
- Respect for others

The first attribute, **confidence** means that you believe in yourself, you trust your own judgment and resourcefulness. We've discussed at length how indispensable confidence is if you want to gain someone's attention.

The second high flexibility attribute is **tolerance**, which means you are open to accepting opinions and practices that are different from your own. We can easily think of people who are *intolerant* of others because of religious or political beliefs. Those intolerant folks may attract like-minded people, but they don't gain the attention of a diverse audience.

The third high flexibility attribute is **empathy.** The root of the word empathy is pathos, which means "feeling" in Greek. Empathy is a term for deep feeling. It means, "I feel what you feel. I can put myself in your shoes." Another word with the same root, sympathy, means merely acknowledging someone else's feelings. It results in kindness and pity, and it comes from the head. Empathy results in feeling the pain, or the joy, of the other person. It comes from the heart.

The fourth high flexibility attribute is **positiveness.** Dr. Norman Vincent Peale's book, *The Power of Positive Thinking*, has sold well for over forty years because it contains such a universal truth. A positive attitude leads to positive events in your life.

The fifth high flexibility characteristic is **respect for others.** This is the sincere desire to understand and consider other people's choices, commitments and needs in relation to yours.

Just think of the successful individuals you have admired, both friends and public figures, and you will probably notice your list is full of people with high flexibility strengths.

Now let's consider the five **Low Flexibility** traits:

- Rigidity
- Competition with others
- Discontent
- Being unapproachable
- Difficulty in dealing with ambiguity.

The first negative flexibility trait, **rigidity**, can be illustrated with the attitude: "It's my way or the highway." It can also come disguised in such sayings as: "That's just the way it is," or "Those are the rules," or "That'll never work." Do those kinds of sayings ever come from your mouth?

Competition is the second low flexibility trait. Competition with others is fine—in sports, in contests for salesperson of the month or in the lottery. But generally, most of our days are spent in collaboration with others, people we work with, live with, and interact with in public. A person who lives his life in competition with everyone—and we all know someone like that—might be admired for his achievements, but he doesn't get the freely given attention and support of others. A person who exudes the message that "I'm smarter, or prettier, or wealthier, or more committed than you are" doesn't garner people's trust. That's because the message is clearly "Me first."

The third negative flexibility trait is **discontent.** This is the opposite of positiveness. In more vernacular terms, a person with this trait is called a complainer, a whiner, a wet blanket. It's easy to see why this person doesn't get support.

Being unapproachable is the fourth negative flexibility trait. Nobody who wants to gain power and influence and with others would describe themselves as "unapproachable." Yet sometimes we hear things like: "I'm sticking to my guns no matter what." Or, "Don't come to me with a problem if you don't have a solution." Or, "I'm only interested in what works." The attitude behind those statements is: "Don't bother me unless it's worth my time and it corresponds to what I already believe." Obviously, this attitude is *not* conducive to collaboration!

The last negative flexibility trait is **difficulty in dealing with ambiguity.** Because ambiguous situations can have several possible meanings, interpretations or outcomes, some people don't like them. For these people, it has to be *either/or,* one way or the other. They get nervous in the face of the unknown. "Let's nail this down." "Let's choose one now and go for it." At times, that approach may be necessary. But rigid people always want to get closure on one meaning, one interpretation, one outcome, as early as possible. And often that approach leaves out the opinions and contributions of other people. It certainly leaves out the possibility of serendipity. On the other hand, people with a high tolerance for ambiguity create more options for good outcomes, including choices they couldn't have predicted.

Now let's look at the other half of the adaptability formula, **versatility**. Our research indicates that people have a better developed level of flexibility than versatility. Versatility requires a set of personal aptitudes. While many people are *willing* to modify their behaviors, they often lack the necessary set of abilities. Versatility is something we acquire over time through a variety of resources. These include formal education, daily life experiences, and observations of others who demonstrate high versatility behaviors. It generally means approaching every situation as a new opportunity for learning and growing.

The five **high versatility** traits are:

- Resilience
- Vision
- Attentiveness
- Competence
- Self-correction

As we look at them one by one, try to honestly assess how much of each ability you possess.

The first high versatility trait, **resilience**, means knowing how to overcome setbacks, barriers and limited resources. Mainly, it has to do with your emotional strength. The very successful Lawrence Kasdan, screenwriter of many hit films including *Raiders of the Lost Ark,* endured over 60 rejections before he finally sold first script.

Could *you* have persevered through dozens of turn-downs? How many cold calls can you make in a row that all turn out to be "No, thank you?" If you keep on going until you succeed, that's resilience.

Vision is the second high versatility trait. I think it's easy to see why someone who has the power to imagine, to be creative, to suggest alternatives, is going to be more influential than someone who can't.

The third high versatility trait is **attentiveness**. That means being aware of elements in the environment. It can be as simple as noticing when someone is getting bored, or sensing that now's not the right time to present your ideas. It is knowing when to act and when not to act. It means paying attention to more than your own needs.

The fourth high versatility trait is **competence**. Competence begins with expertise. It also involves a problem-solving ability that goes beyond your specialty. If you don't know how to answer a question or fix a problem, you can find someone who does. It means having a can-do attitude and following through on it.

The fifth high versatility trait is **self-correction**. That means that once you initiate a project, you ask for feedback and place priority on problem-solving, not on being right. It means you're able to see when you've developed a non-productive pattern in your behavior. It is being able to say: "I think this approach isn't working. I'd better try something different."

Again, the five high versatility traits are: resilience, vision, attentiveness, competence, and self-correction. Now let's round out the picture with the five low versatility attributes: subjectiveness, bluntness, resistance, single-mindedness, and unreasonable risk-taking.

The first negative versatility trait is **subjectiveness**. That means seeing everything strictly from your own perspective. "This is the way it looks to ME." And that's the only way you can look at it. True versatility allows you to see things from other people's perspectives. You may be willing to look at an issue from another perspective, but CAN you do it? In order to reduce your subjectiveness, practice with an issue that you feel strongly about. Can you really articulate the argument of someone on the opposite side?

The next negative versatility trait is **bluntness**. Evaluating someone's idea by saying, "That's stupid!" may be brief and to the point.

But it will cause hurt feelings and a lack of motivation. You can win a lot more people to your side by saying, "You know, this doesn't look like it's going to work. Let's explore some other options that might work better and see if we can incorporate some of your ideas as well." Developing your tact and verbal skills takes time. It is especially helpful to listen to the kinds of phrases that tactful people use: "Let me tell you how I see it," "I know you're feeling strongly about this and I can appreciate that," "Let's see if this fits for you." Tactful people make sure their words don't feel like assault weapons.

The next negative versatility trait is **resistance**. This generally means resistance to change. Obviously, we do not have to accept any and all changes that come down the pike. But every military general, every politician, every medical researcher knows you are dead in the water if you always stick to the "tried and true." Breakthroughs happen when people try something new. If you catch yourself saying: "this is the way we've always done things around here," think about it. What are you resisting?

A fourth negative versatility trait is **single-mindedness**. This is akin to tunnel-vision. It means you have one goal and a set way to achieve it, and nothing else matters. Single-mindedness means you can't see that other people have goals too. Let's recall our discussion of trying to inspire people with a larger vision of what you are seeking, where you help them to see how your plan will fill their needs too. Here is an example of single-mindedness: someone who loves birds so much that she will do anything to protect them. This includes wanting to set out poison for neighboring cats and squirrels. She does not find it in her interest to unite with other people to help all the animals live in a balanced ecosystem; she is only concerned about her beloved birds.

The final negative versatility trait is **unreasonable risk-taking.** If you want to go bungee-jumping and risk your life, that's one thing. But when you are asking people to follow your lead, to go forward on your vision, you need to assess and take responsibility for the risk level that you are creating. How much did John DeLorean assess the risk that his investors were taking by giving him money for his new car company? In retrospect, he was very careless with their money. When you have high versatility, you are able to see a variety of avenues toward the success of your goal, and you choose those with the least amount of risk to those who follow you.

Only when you develop the willingness *and* the ability to adapt can you develop personal power with large numbers of people. You need flexibility and versatility.

In order to test your flexibility and versatility quotients, here's a quiz. In the following pairs of statements decide which one best describes you. Let's begin with flexibility.

Statement A: What do you expect of me? That's just the way I am. It's me, my type of person. I'm stuck with it, so I can't do anything about it.

Statement B: Well, one thing I've learned is that each of us can be our own worst enemy in our own unique way. That's the real benefit I've gained from this type of behavioral style idea. Now I'm aware of my more natural strengths, preferences, and my shortcomings. So I've made a conscious effort to monitor those and make sure they stay in the positive range.

If you answered A, that is an area of low flexibility for you. If B, you have a good foundation for high flexibility.

Here is another pair.

Statement A: Obviously, since no two people are identical, and there are very few Prince Charming/Cinderella matches in the world, each of us has to work at our relationships if we want them to be mutually satisfying. This means I have to be willing to accept every person as worthwhile, regardless of their style. The key is being willing to understand them, as well as accepting them as people I want to get along with. When I do that, I find that things usually work out quite well. When I don't, the relationship suffers. The choice, and the consequences, belongs to me.

Statement B: Look, each of us has our own cross to bear in terms of other people. I can't be expected to get along with everyone. There *are* such things as personality conflicts and that's all there is to it. I try to find those people I get along with and stay away from all those other types that pose problems for me and for themselves too.

This time, A was the high flexibility statement, and B was low flexibility. A highly flexible person is confident, tolerant, empathetic, positive and respectful of others. How do you rate?

Let's review the distinctive abilities of a highly versatile person. This person knows how to productively manage a variety of situations. Their actions are clearly goal-oriented. They are effective in creating desirable outcomes for situations. And they also take appropriate problem-solving actions for dealing with a broad range of situations. On the other hand, a person of low versatility tends to be responsive only to their own preferences or expectations. They also discount the reality of other people's concerns that require consideration. For instance, if someone's behavioral style is direct and supporting, they have difficulty demonstrating behavior that's logical and reserved.

Here is a statement from a person with high versatility: "One of the things I really like about my job is that every day is different. I'm always learning something new, and I have many opportunities to use my talents and develop other ones. In fact, I'm always on the lookout for training that will supplement my abilities and benefit my career.

A statement from a low versatility person might sound like this: "I hate work. It's always the same old thing, day after day, year after year. The only really good thing about it is I get a chance to meet many people and get invited to a lot of great parties. I don't think I need to learn anything new in order to keep my job.

Which statement sound like you? Low versatility people are trapped in a rut. They may be willing to improve themselves, but they are not confident about their ability to do so. They have not developed their capabilities in many areas.

Doing your own assessment of how versatile you are is tough. Ask your friends, your spouse, your boss, and your kids if they think you have what it takes to succeed in a wide variety of situations. If they say you display some low-versatility characteristics, ask them to elaborate. Above all, do not get defensive! You are taking a survey, not looking for an argument.

If you do that survey, you might discover that you are not as versatile as you might think. The good news is you do not have to be a prisoner of your own behavior patterns and tendencies. You can choose whether you will be a person with higher or lower flexibility and versatility.

The bad news is that changing those patterns does not happen overnight, or without occasional regressions to the old behaviors you felt more comfortable with. You can speed up the process and increase your probability for success by focusing once again on your personal behavioral style. It means reviewing the negative characteristics of your type that we covered in the previous segments. It also means making a commitment to work toward overcoming those behaviors. Taking the time to determine how direct or indirect you are, and how supporting or controlling you are, will improve your relationships and your persuasion ability with others.

Developing power adaptability allows you to speak many different "behavior style languages" and understand how different types of people would like to be treated. If you choose to use this ability, you increase your personal power and motivate others to achieve your objectives. You also help them achieve their own objectives.

Communication Adaptability involves making strategic adjustments to your methods of communicating and behaving. It is based on the particular needs of the relationship at a particular time. Adaptable people make the choice to go beyond their own comfort zone so that others feel more comfortable. As I have said before, adaptability does not mean imitating the other person's behavior. It *does* mean adjusting your own behavior to be more in line with the other person's preference. At the same time, it means maintaining your own identity, good sense and basic values.

Your adaptability level affects the way other people perceive you. When you raise your adaptability, trust and credibility go up; lowered and trust and credibility go down. Communication adaptability means allowing others to be more at ease, encouraged and successful in a relationship with you. It concerns the way you manage your communication and actions. It also involves how you manage the requirements that exist for a task or situation. In a given situation, you can choose to be adaptable with one person and not with another. You can also choose to be quite adaptable with one person today, and less so with that same person tomorrow.

Finally, people often adopt a somewhat different role in their professional lives than they do in their personal lives. You may tend to be more adaptable at work because you want to create a good impression. But at home, you may relax and act "more yourself," which may be less adaptable. People with power and influence understand that adaptability is important in *both* personal and professional relationships, and that one person is just as important as another.

Another way of looking at this whole matter is from the perspective of maturity. Mature people know who they are. They don't place a priority on one area of their life at the expense of another. And whenever problems or opportunities arise, they are willing and able to meet the need. Immature people, on the other hand, pay attention only to their own needs, and disregard the needs of others. This causes conflict and tension, which leads to less satisfaction and less effectiveness in every aspect of their lives.

In this chapter, I asked you to rate yourself in the areas of flexibility and versatility. Let's review the characteristics: The high flexibility characteristics include confidence, tolerance, empathy, positiveness and respect for others.

The low flexibility characteristics are rigidity, competition with others, discontent, being unapproachable and having difficulty dealing with ambiguity. The high versatility characteristics are resilience, vision, attentiveness, competence and self-correction. The low versatility characteristics are subjectiveness, bluntness, resistance to change, single-mindedness, and unreasonable risk-taking.

The mix you have of these characteristics plays a strong role in your ability to communicate effectively. That's why it is so important to do an honest appraisal of your willingness and ability to adapt your behavior.

I think it is impossible to determine your score on those 20 adaptability traits by yourself. That's why I suggest you do a survey with family, friends and coworkers. Remember, you are looking for honest answers, not an argument. When you adopt the willingness *and* the ability to adapt, you will gain one more quality of the World's Greatest Communicators.

How to Use Space and Time to Your Communication Advantage

The ninth quality of the World's Greatest Communicators is an important skill to master. The way you use space and time sends important communication signals, whether you intend to or not. This chapter will show you how to communicate more skillfully and proactively through your use of space and time, and how to understand the signals others send you through their use of space and time.

We are territorial creatures, whether we are talking about space or time. Virtually every day, you and I are affected by how these two powerful communication tools are used. For example, if you violate someone's physical comfort zone by standing too close to them, or sitting in the wrong place, or touching them when they think you shouldn't, you may offend them and cause tension. Similarly, if you abuse another person's sense of time—by being too late or too early, for example, or by leaving too quickly or staying too long—you can cause tension.

On the other hand, you can enhance your communication effectiveness by staying flexible and being aware of the time and spatial needs of others. When you decide where someone should sit when they enter your office, or when you limit what distractions can intrude on your meeting, you can actively set a tone and send out a positive message.

The first step in communicating skillfully through space and time is recognizing the dynamics of something called proxemics, which is defined as space and the movement of people within it. You may already be familiar with some aspects of this relationship.

For instance, have you ever had someone stand so close to you that you felt threatened or uncomfortable? Or, how do you feel when you return to a meeting after a break and find someone else is sitting in "your place"? The uncomfortable feelings most of us experience in these situations result from violations of our personal space.

Let's talk about territoriality. Your reactions to the questions about someone crowding you or taking your seat are probably consistent with the conclusion of anthropologists that human beings are territorial animals with inherent compulsions to possess and defend space as exclusive property. For instance, when you enter a meeting, you establish your territory, bounded by movable objects such as your notebook, coffee cup, and the jacket hanging on your chair. Although you have no legal rights to certain geographic areas just because you arrived there first and staked out your claim with your possessions, your immediate reaction to returning to the meeting and finding someone else in your seat is probably a feeling of loss, followed possibly by anger and a desire to regain your space.

It is important to remember that people like to protect and control their territory. Respecting, rather than violating this, can enhance the delivery of your message. Of course, controlling and protecting is easier to do with fixed feature territories, where it is possible to shut your door or even lock it. In semi-fixed feature territories, the best protection is your physical presence. If you are absent for a while, your only protection is other people's respect for honoring your territory. If it is a desirable territory, you may return and find that someone else has claimed it.

There are times when others invade even our fixed feature territory or cause us to lose control over it. This is a more severe social violation than ignoring semi-fixed boundaries, and your angry feelings are apt to be even greater. If you have your door closed and someone walks into your office without knocking and without being invited, the tension between you increases. Similar reactions would probably occur if a visitor sits in your chair, uses your pen, or grabs your personal appointment book to check a date for a future meeting.

Remember, other people would have the same negative reactions to these kinds of behaviors as you would. Therefore, in attempting to establish a good working relationship with co-workers or employees, don't violate their territory, even if you are the boss. When dealing with territory, mutual respect is the norm, and mutual trust is based on honoring it. People value their privacy and need to protect and control their personal territory. Studies have even demonstrated that if you are talking to someone and inadvertently violate some aspect of his personal space, he may be so upset that he doesn't hear another word you say.

Knowing that people react to issues about their space, there are several ways to utilize feelings about territory and environment to enhance communication and relationships. For example, it is always best, to arrange for meetings in an attractive location so that participants will feel comfortable and important. If they enjoy their surroundings, they will probably have more desire to continue their activities and do a good job worthy of the setting. The meeting place should, of course, be a neutral location so that territorial problems won't intimidate those who are meeting on another's turf. Finally, flexible seating is encouraged to allow participants to establish their own semi-fixed territories and appropriate spatial arrangements.

If a supervisor wants to establish more intimacy in relationships with employees, it sometimes helps to have one-to-one meetings in employees' offices or in a neutral place. The supervisor needs to also apply appropriate body language during the conversation. Standing or leaning over someone who is seated conveys power and can be intimidating and uncomfortable for the person sitting. On the other hand, leaning back and appearing too casual can also convey a feeling of superiority and create a negative reaction in the employee.

Even the way you arrange your office furniture communicates the degree of formality you wish to maintain in your interactions with visitors. If your chair is behind your desk, you create a barrier between you and your visitors, and may result in relatively short and formal interactions. A chair closer to the visitor, without the barrier of a desk, creates a much more informal and relaxed atmosphere, which encourages longer and more open interactions.

Whether we mean to or not, the air space around us is another aspect of space we use to communicate. We assume that this is our personal territory, much like a private air bubble. We feel a proprietary right to this space and resent others entering it unless we invite them in. The exact dimensions of these private bubbles vary from culture to culture and with different personality styles. The following generalities can help you understand the dynamics of these private spaces so you can better use them to receive and send messages.

Research in proxemics reveals that adult American business people have four basic distances of interaction. They are the **Intimate Zone**, which ranges from actual physical contact to about two feet; the **Personal Zone**, which ranges from approximately two feet to four feet in distance; the **Social Zone** that extends from nearly four feet to roughly twelve feet; and the **Public Zone** that stretches from twelve feet away to the limits of hearing and sight.

People are not necessarily conscious of the importance of maintaining these distances until violations occur, which can easily lead to increased tension.

How you feel about people entering these different zones depends upon who they are. You might feel quite uncomfortable and resentful if a business associate enters your Intimate or Personal Zone during a conversation. Manager/employee relationships usually begin in the Social Zone of four to twelve feet. Often, they move to the Personal Zone over time after a high level of trust has developed. The trick is to know when this time is and not move into this space too soon.

You should be aware that people can generally be classified into two major proxemics categories—contact and non-contact. According to Edward Hall, those of Northern European descent are typically in the non-contact group due to the small amount of touching that takes place during their transactions. Of course, there are exceptions. On the other hand, Arabs and Latins normally use much contact in their conversations. Contact and non-contact people can have conflicting perceptions of each other based solely on their proxemics behavior. The contact people see the non-contact people as shy, cold, and impolite. On the other hand, non-contact people perceive contact people as pushy, aggressive, and impolite.

When a proxemics violation occurs, whether someone is felt to be too close or too distant, the person sensing this may generally have a feeling that something is not right, even if they can't quite determine what it is. This can cause attention to naturally shift away from the conversation at hand, creating a breakdown in effective communication.

Personality is a factor in proxemics. Extroverts prefer closer interpersonal distances than do introverts. Individuals who feel like they have control over their lives, tend to like closer distances to others than do people who feel as though their lives are controlled externally. With respect to learning style, some people prefer working closely with others, whereas others prefer distance and minimal contact.

Previous relationships also determine arrangements. People who have interacted successfully with each other in the past prefer closer distances than individuals who do not feel comfortable with each other.

When it comes to gender, it should come as no surprise that men and women like to be closer to others of the opposite sex than to others of the same sex. However, when interacting with members of the same sex, females tend to tolerate less space between them than do males when they are interacting with other males. Research has demonstrated that male employees permit female supervisors to get closer to them than male supervisors. For female employees, there was no difference in the space they permit between themselves and their supervisors, whether female or male.

You can learn a lot about what the use of personal space means to you by being aware of your own behavior and by noticing how you feel about your own space and how you react to others who behave differently. With this knowledge, you can become more skillful at communicating your message to others as well as understanding what others are saying to you.

In attempting to build trust, be careful not to offend a person by intruding on their proxemics zones or territory. This is especially true if you are a supervisor or a manager because employees may feel like they had no recourse to the intrusion. There are many consequences for violating the proxemics rules of behavior, including an increase in tension, a decrease in credibility, and a reduced chance of gaining commitment or agreement.

Understanding the concepts of proxemics helps you avoid negative consequences and enhances the communication process with everyone you encounter. This is especially important in the supervisor-employee relationship because that unequal-power relationship is often subject to tension, conflict, and mistrust. The supervisory process has been described as initially meeting the employee face-to-face at a social distance and slowly moving to a side-by-side personal distance. This move happens only as trust is built. Care should be exercised in not moving too fast, which will increase tension, or too slow, which could indicate rejection. Good communicators respect, understand, and effectively use the concepts of proxemics. The payoff is more attention, more trust, better communication, and a better chance for productive working relationships.

Now, let's turn to what your use of time says to other people. Consider these scenarios:

- How do you feel when you are kept waiting for an appointment to discuss something with your boss?
- Or when a colleague or employee is chronically late to meetings?
- How about when someone arrives early for a meeting with you?
- What is your reaction when your boss stops talking with you as much as usual and begins spending more time with a co-worker?

These examples demonstrate how the use of time communicates how someone else feels about them—especially feelings related to their status and importance and to being liked. Time is a scarce resource. Be aware that whomever you give it to, how much you give, and when you give it, communicate your feelings about others.

Professor Anthony Athos has identified three major variables we use to assign meaning to time. They include **accuracy, scarcity,** and **repetition.**

In our western culture, concern for time accuracy is enormous. Watches are advertised as not being more than a few seconds off a year, and we literally strap them to our bodies so that we can know exactly what time it is so we are able to stay precisely on schedule. Because of this concern for accuracy, deviations in how we use our time communicate a powerful message to other people.

It's not uncommon for a manager to assume that an employee who is frequently late to department meetings doesn't care, and that manager may well get angry at this perceived indifference. Employees also tend to assume that managers who are late to meetings also don't care much. Consequently, how accurate we are with time often broadcasts a message about our level of caring, even if that is not the message we intend. So, a word to the wise is to be punctual.

Time can also be used to tell others how we feel about them in terms of their relative status and power. If the president of the company calls a junior manager to her office for a meeting, the manager will probably arrive before the appointed time. Because of the difference in status, most managers would probably feel that any inconvenience in waiting ought to be theirs. The president's time is regarded as worth more and, therefore, is not to be wasted.

Time use is also a mechanism for defining relationships. If two managers of equal status are very competitive, one might try to structure the other's time to demonstrate greater status and power. Here's how this could play out. One manager calls the other and asks him to come to his office for a meeting later that morning. First, the initiation to have a meeting indicates a higher status. Second, specifying the place and time diminishes the other's influence. Third, the immediacy of the intended meeting implies that the other has nothing more important to do. If the second manager agrees to the meeting, the chances are high that this manager will not arrive for the meeting exactly on time. The silent message is: "My time is equal to yours, and I'm at least equal to you."

Using time to manipulate or control others is common, although we are not usually aware of it, whether we are on the initiating or the receiving end. When we allow others to structure our time, it is usually in deference to their relative greater status or power.

But even if there is an unbalance of power, in general, the longer a person is kept waiting, the more stroking is required to neutralize the feelings of hostility that gathered during the waiting period. If you can become aware of this process, it can help you understand your feelings better when you are the person who is waiting. It also can increase your skill at helping others not feel put down when they have to wait for you because of some legitimate commitment.

The second variable we use to assign meaning to time is scarcity. Time and money are two of our most limited resources. However, while we can often work harder or smarter and make more money, there is nothing we can do to change the amount of time we get. Each of us has the same amount. How and with whom we spend it communicates what and whom we value. If we choose to spend time going to a little league game rather than working overtime, it is a signal about what we think is important. If we choose to spend time perfecting the budget rather than listening to an employee's problem, that too sends a message. We are constantly broadcasting to the world our likes and dislikes by how we use our time.

For example, you may find you need to spend a greater amount of time than usual with a particular employee or co-worker because of a new procedure or special problem. If this causes your time with other co-workers to be temporarily reduced, they may feel that you care more about that person and project and less about them and their projects.

The "cost" of your time varies from moment to moment, depending on how much you have to do and how much time you have to do it in. Communications may be strained, for example, when you're in a big hurry to complete a report and a co-worker drops in to chat for a while. This type of tension can affect a relationship if it is seen as non-caring. The tension can be avoided by explaining your situation and why you are in a hurry. It also helps to make a date in the future to make up the time if necessary.

In general, since time is viewed as a scarce resource, the way we spend it is often taken as a signal of who we care about. Being aware of this can help you build more productive relationships by simply stating out loud what the meaning is for the way your time is spent. It can prevent others from jumping to the wrong conclusions and prevent you from having your own feelings hurt.

Time also has meaning for us in its **repetition** of activities. Most of us become irritated when someone interrupts a pattern we have become accustomed to, such as missing a customary 10:00 a.m. coffee break or needing to work late and miss dinner with your family.

Our reactions to the seasons—another pattern of time—and how we use them also varies. People become accustomed to certain activities and feelings associated with different seasons and holidays. For example, there is usually less work done during the Christmas holidays, and trying to get people to work overtime during this season can be deeply resented.

Any disruption of established patterns of activities will be experienced as a deprivation, and if you are perceived as the source of the disruption, hostile feelings will be directed your way. Use care when planning changes in workload, especially during holiday seasons and use your questioning skills to determine unique individual patterns and expectations.

Although the accuracy, scarcity, and repetition of time vary from one situation to another, your use of time to communicate speaks very loudly.

Because use of time is such an expressive language, being aware of its various meanings can facilitate your communications and relationships with others. This is especially true for managers because of the tendencies of employees to watch them intensely for nonverbal feedback.

The rules regarding time are simple and well known, although they aren't followed as often as they should be. In order to avoid negative communications through your use of time, be punctual. Let others know if you can't meet a prearranged time commitment. Don't keep people waiting but, if you do, plan to deal with their feelings of anger about the wait. In addition, don't impose unusual schedules that will obviously conflict with personal schedules or holidays. Don't change the amount of time you spend with a person without giving them a reason for the change. It is just common sense that being considerate with our use of time and openly stating the reasons for time changes can go a long way in avoiding misunderstandings and building more trusting and productive relationships. And that leads to greater levels of communication.

Energy and Aura

The tenth and final quality of the World's Greatest Communicators is especially important. Energy and Aura are significant attributes since the communicator is always part of the message. A great communicator knows this and uses it to his or her advantage.

A noteworthy example of this is Ronald Reagan, known as "The Great Communicator." When he spoke, audiences were drawn in by his smile and approachable demeanor. His nonverbal communication was as powerful as his verbal message, helping people relate on a personal level. We are drawn to high-energy people because of their enthusiasm and passion.

People who possess this enthusiasm and passion are able to maintain an excitement about them that lasts far beyond a favorable first impression. They are able to maintain that energy long after the stimulation of temporary situations such as presentations or performances, is over. The people who possess genuine sustained enthusiasm and passion are able to attract and influence people because they project their best possible selves. They know how to establish bonds with people that are based on respect and honest communication. Those are the areas of focus in this chapter.

Let me give you a way to think about enthusiasm and passion, this magnetic energy that is so important to personal persuasion and communication. I think of it as an invisible rainbow surrounding you. The "colors" of this rainbow are different aspects of who you are. These aspects include your physical self, your emotional self, your psychological self, your intellectual self, your strategic self and your spiritual self.

Just as white light going through a prism separates into the colors we see in a rainbow, we can imagine your whole self being refracted into the six aspects of enthusiasm and passion.

Some rainbows emphasize certain colors more than others do. It is the same with people in the kinds of energy we give off. I think we may agree that the best rainbows are the ones where you can see all the colors in vibrant hues.

The first color in your energy rainbow comes from your **physical self**. This includes how you look, your grooming, your posture, your smile, and perhaps most significantly, your fitness. I am sure I do not need to convince anybody that when you are feeling physically fit you are going to come across well to others. We are all attracted to healthy-looking people. It is one of the pleasures of watching top athletes.

Fitness is not mysterious. It is made up of three primary components, strength, flexibility and aerobic ability. A person can be good in one or two areas, say strength and aerobics, but stiff as a board as far as flexibility goes. Or there are those who can bench press 200 pounds and curl into yoga pretzels, but gasp for breath after running a half a block.

Real fitness means having some capacity in all three areas: you have reasonable strength for your size and age, you can sustain aerobic exercise for 20 minutes three times a week, and your body has sufficient flexibility.

Another important aspect of your physical energy has to do with diet. In the past 20 years or so, most of us have picked up valuable information about the role of such things as vitamins, fiber and fats in our everyday eating. Let me tell you a quick personal story. It has to do with the role of sugar in my diet. I've discovered that when I eat too much sugar, I might get an initial rush of energy, but after that, I feel dull, I react more slowly, I move more slowly. If I've had too much sugar the night before, usually in the form of desserts, I feel groggy in the morning.

Recently, I tried an experiment and went off sugar completely for three days. Even though I only slept 7 hours the first night, I woke up in the morning feeling ready to go. It is really clear to me that I compromise my energy level if I eat too much sugar. As I said earlier, one of the most magnetic components of personal power is a high level of energy. I can tell you from personal experience that sugar slows you down.

A word to the wise for coffee drinkers too—coming at someone with *too much* energy can be off-putting. If you drink a lot of coffee, get feedback from your colleagues about whether you get too intense or talk too fast after that third cup. Sometimes we are just not aware of how our behavior changes based on what we eat.

Let's consider your **emotional energy** next. For our purposes, we will look at three components of this quality, although you may feel there are many more. We'll concentrate on passion, enthusiasm and a positive attitude toward life.

The late Luciano Pavarotti told the story of how, when he was growing up in Italy, he was an average singer in the boy's church choir. The only reason he was allowed to stay was because his father was choirmaster. He said he had one image in his mind from the very beginning. He wanted to be the only person in his country who was spoken about with the same reverence as they spoke about Enrico Caruso, an internationally revered opera singer from the previous generation. Pavarotti studied, practiced, trained, and envisioned himself at the pinnacle of the opera world and he certainly made his passion come true.

What do you feel passionate about? You will never influence anyone to change their ideas or take action if you do not feel strongly about it yourself.

Enthusiasm is another component of your emotional energy. Your enthusiasm is communicated in your face, your voice and your gestures. Sometimes we *feel* enthusiasticly about our ideas but are afraid to show it.

Enthusiastic, passionate people are those who are able to project their best possible *inner* and *outer* selves. I think the people who influence us the most are those who are able to express on the outside what they are feeling on the inside.

Your *passion* is WHAT you care about. Your *enthusiasm* stems from WHY you care about it. The better you are able to express WHY you care about something, the more you will find other people getting enthusiastic about it too.

The third component of your emotional self is a **positive attitude** toward life. Dr. Norman Vincent Peale published a book in 1952 about the power of positive thinking, and it continues to sell and sell to this very day. We all need to be reminded from time to time that our mental attitude colors and shapes reality for us. Do you tend to view your life as half full, in that you have much to be grateful for and room for improvement? Or do you tend to view your life as half empty, in that it is missing many things and you will always be stuck in a life of quiet desperation? With the first view, you attract success and happiness in your life, and with the second, you are faced with disappointment time and time again.

The important thing to remember is that you are not born with attitudes. Positive and negative attitudes develop over time as a response to life events. Individual attitudes add up and create a lens through which you view reality. As time goes by, you develop specific attitudes toward people, politics, foods, parts of the world and parts of your own body.

If your overall attitude is cheerful, hopeful, and tolerant of differences, you convey a positive attitude toward life. On the other hand, if your attitude is critical, pessimistic and intolerant of anything unfamiliar, you convey a negative attitude toward life. Guess which attitude gets better results when you are trying to influence people?

Another reason why a positive attitude is important is that it supports you when the going gets rough. We can only imagine how many young people n in difficult life situations have dreamed of becoming professional athletes. Isaiah Thomas made it while thousands of others did not. I am sure he faced many difficult days as a young athlete, days when it seemed impossible. His positive attitude, reinforced by his mother's faith in him, carried him to the top. He acknowledges that it took both of them believing he could do it to get him there.

The third aspect of your energy rainbow is your **psychological self**. There is a big overlap between the emotional and the psychological, but for our purposes let's define emotional as how you *feel* about yourself and your goals, and psychological as how you *think* about them. Do you think about your goals as achievable? Do you think about yourself as a can-do person? When you're involved in a group project, do you consider yourself an asset to the group, or just one of the workers?

Dr. Nathaniel Branden defines self- esteem as the sum of self-confidence and self-respect. For him, self-confidence is knowing that you have what it takes to function reasonably well in the world. You feel competent to make choices, to satisfy your needs, to chart the course of your life. Confidence in specific situations, such as when you're attempting to influence someone, would flow from a general self-confidence in your abilities.

According to Dr. Branden, self-respect is the second component of self-esteem. This is the feeling of self-worth. You feel that you deserve to be happy and have the love and respect of other people; that your presence in a group is an asset; that what you value deserves attention from other people.

Self-esteem is not what others think of you, it is what you think of yourself. It has nothing to do with material possessions or popularity or how good looking you are. It is simply whether you think of yourself as a competent and worthwhile person.

Dr. Branden lists a number of tip-offs to a person's level of self-esteem. Someone with high self-esteem is able to speak of accomplishments *and* shortcomings with directness and honesty. This person is comfortable giving and receiving compliments, and can express affection and appreciation.

People who suffer from low self-esteem are ruled by fears. They are afraid of the judgments of other people, afraid they are not fit for the challenges of life. They do not explore their own inner world for fear of finding undesirable feelings or facts about themselves.

It is pretty easy to see how your psychological self directly affects your ability to influence and gain power with other people. The message that you are a competent and worthwhile person begins with you. You convey that message with your face, your gestures, the way you talk and the way you hold your body.

A healthy psychological self can be a tremendous asset. It is definitely worth the time it takes to do an honest assessment of what you think about yourself. Sometimes you have to do a mental spring cleaning to get rid of negative thoughts that have become ingrained attitudes.

Let me ask you this: do you find yourself often beginning a thought with these phrases: "I could never. . . ." Or, "I'm terrible at . . ." Stopping self-destructive thoughts is similar to stopping any other bad habit. It takes time and conscious effort.

One of the most effective ways to eliminate negative thoughts about yourself is the use of affirmations, which are positive statements about yourself that you repeat over and over in your head until they are programmed into your subconscious.

If you catch yourself saying: "I'm terrible at remembering names," stop and immediately say to yourself: "I'm good at remembering names." Affirmations may not *feel* true at first. They may not *be* true!

But anything you say to yourself over and over will actually influence your reality. You have everything to gain by talking to yourself positively.

The fourth aspect of your personal energy comes from how well you have developed the thinking apparatus inside your skull. This is your **intellectual self**. I'm not talking about high IQs or your ability to win at Trivial

Pursuit. I am referring to the depth and breadth of your knowledge.

We are all aware of the importance of exercising our bodies, especially as we get older. It should be no surprise that exercise is vital for our brains too. The three aspects of physical fitness that we discussed apply to mental fitness as well, and those are strength, flexibility and aerobic ability. Can your mind lift abstract concepts from *The Wall Street Journal* or from the professional journal in your field? Can you grasp the intricacies of a problem explained by someone in a field completely different than your own? That's mental strength.

Can you see an issue from a perspective that's 180 degrees from your own feelings? Can you entertain ideas that come from a different culture or from people you don't like? That's mental flexibility.

Can you hang in there when it is going to take a lot of convincing to get people to see things your way? When it means clearing seven committees *and* the CEO? Do you have the stamina to read that report tonight instead of vegging out in front of the TV? That is mental aerobic ability.

Training your mind to take on longer and more demanding tasks gives you the stamina you need when mental marathons come up. Most of us were given plenty of basic intelligence. We decide whether we will use it to capacity or let it get flabby and stiff from disuse.

The next aspect of the enthusiasm and passion rainbow is related to the intellectual, but it has an energy all its own. This is your **strategic self**. Two skills are important here: how to set goals and how to "chunk" big projects into manageable pieces. Let's start with goal-setting. When you are attempting to influence someone, you must be able to paint a picture or suggest a plan of action that makes commitment seem reasonable. In other words, you must present a strategy or a series of goals.

I have found that the letters in the word SMART are very useful in articulating goals. SMART reminds me that my goals must be Specific, Measurable, Attainable, Realistic and Trackable. Specific and measurable relate to how you word your goal. Instead of "I will be healthier in six months than I am now," you say "In six months my resting blood pressure will be ten points lower." Or, "In six months I will be twenty pounds lighter." Being specific and measurable makes the goal more motivating. "I will be running three miles in four to six months" is more effective than saying: "I'll be running more in four to six months."

Attainable and Realistic have to do with the goal itself. A goal should have an 80% chance of being accomplished. Anything with a lower chance of becoming reality is often demotivating. On the other hand, a goal with 100% chance of achievement is not really a goal. The purpose of goals is to make you work harder, or to gather more resources than you have in the past. It must move you forward. Something that is a certainty is not a goal, it's a given. It is necessary to set goals that are attainable yet challenging.

SMART goal-setting is Trackable. How will you know if you are making progress? You need to set up a tracking system that details interim goals or checkpoints along the way. Depending on what your goal is, you might be checking your progress every day, once a week, or once every two months. You may discover that your goal is not attainable or realistic within the time frame you've given it. Be flexible about your game plan before you reconsider your goal. Nothing ever goes exactly according to plan, so you may have to make adjustments in order to stay on track and keep up your motivation.

Another aspect of your strategic self is knowing how to break large tasks into smaller ones. I use the word "chunking" to describe this process. Here's an example of how this process works. When I landed a contract to write my first book, *Non-Manipulative Selling*, I had six months to write it. On my "To Do" list every day of those six months was: Write book. Six months went by, no book. The publisher gave me another three months. Three months of "Write book" on my "To Do" list. No book. Finally, the publisher gave me a final three months or else I'd lose the contract.

Fortunately, Karl Albrecht, author of *Service America*, gave me the concept of "chunking." He asked me how many pages I had to write. I said 180. How many days to write it? I answered 90. So he said every day on my "To Do" list should have this note: Write 2 pages of book. I *had* to write two pages; but if I got on a roll, I could write four or five. But the next day I still had to write two. By following his advice, I finished the book in 30 days!

One final technique for managing your strategic energy comes from John Lee, an expert in time management. He says when a new task crops up, or an old one reemerges, apply one of the four "D's": Drop it, Delegate it, Delay it or Do it. Consciously choosing one of those strategies every time you face a task will keep things progressing smoothly.

Let's distinguish between your intellectual self and your strategic self so you can assess your own strengths and determine where you need to focus attention. You may be strong in the intellectual department—you are able to grasp concepts, look at issues from a variety of angles and keep pursuing something that requires endless hours of work. But you may be weak in determining your strategy—setting up *the process* for taking something from A to Z. On the other hand, you may be one of those great process people—"give me a project and I'll make it happen." But you may *not* be great when it comes to negotiating the compromises that inevitably need to be made when you are trying to influence a large group of people.

Now I would like to touch briefly on the sixth aspect of your enthusiasm and passion rainbow—your **spiritual self**. By spiritual I mean things like the bond of trust you are able to create with another person, the level of caring and attitude of service you convey to the person or group you are trying to influence and the sense of higher purpose or greater good that you communicate as part of your vision. This aspect of self is the dynamic between two people in the arena of persuasion and effective communication.

Let me tell you a story in which spiritual energy was the key to positively influencing a large number of people in regard to a very negative turn of events. David Lelewer was handed a job in 1982 that nobody wanted. As head of Human Resources at Levi Strauss Corporation, he led the task force in charge of downsizing the faltering clothing company. In its 100 year history, Levi Strauss was known as the company that cared about its people.

He had to convince the 10,000 people who were laid off and the 30,000 who remained that this was best for everyone. Lelewer brought the workers together in groups to discuss the situation. He hired therapists and job counselors for the people to talk with. The company provided generous severance pay and continued health benefits, and they helped people find other jobs. The humane way Lelewer handled the situation became a model for industries across the country.

We have seen the importance of natural energy and developing that unmistakable aura of success. By increasing these attributes, we can turn on our personal power. Enthusiastic, passionate people attract the confidence of others because they have confidence in themselves, and gaining this confidence is key in becoming a great communicator.

Summary: Putting It All Together

I f you want to make this book better than a good read, the real trick is moving from agreement, into action, and to making changes that last. Grandma Moses said it well: "Life is what we make it. Always has been, always will be."

Serious learners cultivate personal change. Now is the time to acknowledge and reward your own change efforts, because if change is possible, it is time to start making those changes today. There isn't one particular silver bullet that will make you the great communicator you want to become. Mastery is the result of sustained dedication and focused application.

Your future as a great communicator depends on many things, but it mostly depends on *you*. Decide now to claim your own title as one of the world's great communicators.

At a certain point in your life, there are more yesterdays than tomorrows. In fact, you never know when that point passes; so I believe you want to spend your tomorrows carefully on changes worth making. My commitment to you is that this closing chapter will not be just a summary or another goal setting exercise.

Let's start by triggering your memory of some of the key points on great communications I've shared with you in the previous chapters. Take time while going through the following review and use a blank piece of paper to capture phrases or insights that are important to you. You want short entries without long explanations.

On your path to becoming a great communicator, you need to master the art of Asking Questions. This skill helps you gain the information you need, build trust, stimulate the views and opinions of others, and verify information. You use closed questions to gather facts, such as "What color do you prefer," or "Does this seem right so far." Open questions are used to draw out a wide range of responses on a broad topic and often ask for opinions, thoughts or feelings. This type of question is effective in stimulating thinking about your ideas, as well as giving you insight into what others are thinking or feeling.

The second quality to work on is becoming a great Listener. Active listening is as powerful as speech, and ineffective listening is one of the most frequent causes of misunderstandings, mistakes and problems. I gave you six skills that can help you become a great listener. They formed the acronym CARESS, which stands for concentrate, acknowledge, research, exercise emotional control, sense the nonverbal message and structure. When you become an active listener, you will have fewer communication glitches, your relationships will improve, and in business settings, productivity and morale will go up in your organization.

In our chapter on Feedback, I stressed the point that this skill may very well be the most important aspect of interpersonal communications if a conversation is to continue for any length of time and still have meaning for the parties involved. Good feedback, both verbal and nonverbal, can reduce interpersonal tension, while clarifying messages and uncovering important needs or problems. To help improve the accuracy and clarity of a message during a conversation you could use verbal statements such as, "Let me be sure I understand what you've said." Reading nonverbal feedback is essential because people use their bodies, eyes, faces, postures, and senses, to communicate a variety of positive or negative attitudes, feelings, and opinions, many of which may contradict what they are saying verbally. If you are "deaf" to a person's nonverbal message, you may not hear what is actually being communicated.

In chapter four I explained how you can harness your powers of Concentration and Focus in order to send and receive messages effectively. This is necessary because of the external and internal barriers to effective communication. External barriers are mostly environmental, such as competing noises in a crowded restaurant, but they can involve the speaker themselves—an accent or pace of delivery. Internal barriers typically have to do with the physical state of the listener: being tired, for example.

To overcome these barriers I gave you four techniques: breath in deeply, decide to listen, mentally paraphrase what is being said, and maintain eye contact. By exercising your ability to focus, you will learn to overcome communication barriers, which is a major step in becoming a great communicator.

The next key point is to develop a strong Memory because of the impression it will have on people. Hopefully, you recall that memory is a trait you can develop and improve, just as you can get better at running or swimming. You can work at it and control it and then benefit from that work. Throughout the ages, a good memory has been viewed as a sign of greater intelligence. The truth is, anyone can develop a strong memory, but the perception still exists. So why not develop your memory and leverage that perception to gain more respect as a communicator. Come to think of it, although it is true that smarter people do not innately have stronger memories, it is the smart ones who chose to develop strong memories.

In the chapter covering the art of Conflict Resolution, I helped you understand how to encourage healthy disagreement without spiraling down into a negative conflict. Productive disagreement of ideas and opinions leads to new ideas and better solutions and action plans. The conflict management options we covered were avoidance, accommodation, domination, negotiation, collaboration, and confrontation. To help resolve conflict in almost any situation you encounter, I offered five basic behaviors. They are, project an attitude of openness, listen with empathy, demonstrate supportiveness, have an attitude of positiveness, and treat the other people and their ideas and opinions as equal. Keep in mind that although most people view conflict as something negative, conflict can offer many benefits when resolved productively.

The power of being a great Presenter was the topic of our seventh chapter. The ability to make public presentations is the number one predictor of the level of professional success, and yet, it is the number one fear of most adults. If this includes you, revisit this session because I offered many tips for overcoming stage fright. Building on that, I discussed the characteristics of an effective speaker, which include understanding the needs of an audience, being the expert on a subject, being enthusiastic about the subject, plus many more. I also stressed the importance of preparation since the success of your public speaking is determined primarily by the time you spend preparing before you step in front of your audience.

Next, I talked about being Highly Adaptable. It will serve you well to master an attitude of being Flexible, and the aptitude to be Versatile to make adaptability work in continually shaping your future. That reminds me of what Neil Postman said in his book, *We Are Amusing Ourselves to Death*. He said, "We come into school a question mark, and we leave a period." School often teaches us to accept one answer, not to entertain options. Adaptability is about embracing options so we can change our approach depending on the situation or individual we are dealing with.

The next chapter focused on Using Space and Time. How you use these two elements sends important signals. For example, if you violate someone else's physical comfort zone by standing too close to them or by sitting in the wrong place, you may offend them and cause tension. Similarly, if you abuse another person's sense of time—by being too late or too early, or by leaving too quickly or staying too long—you could also cause tension. Understanding the rules of space and time can go a long way in avoiding misunderstandings and building more trusting and productive relationships, which lead to greater levels of communication.

In the final chapter we began with a focus on developing Energy and Aura. This is important since the communicator is always part of the message. People with high energy naturally draw others to themselves, creating a heightened receptivity for their message. This energy and aura are like the colors of a rainbow, producing many aspects of who you are, including your physical self, emotional self, psychological self, intellectual self, strategic self and spiritual self. The great communicators are the ones who emit all of these "colors" in vibrant hues that project a personal power that in turn, attracts the confidence of others.

Did that review trigger the insights, or keepers, that mean the most to you? Of course, you want more than insights—you want changes that last.

Research suggests that relapse rates—in other words, our tendency to return to old habits—can be as high as

90 percent. It doesn't have to happen with this program. Zig Ziglar said this about personal change: "The biggest person standing in your way is you. Others can stop you temporarily—you're the only one who can do it permanently."

Don't let that happen. Don't put this away until you have isolated *your* Keepers—the key points that you've found most valuable and worth establishing in your daily life.

You want to find the learning nuggets that are critical to ensuring your personal change. What we know about learning and change is very clear: without focused review, clear goals and a workable plan, you are unlikely to retain the information or change your habits.

As Yogi Berra said, "If you don't know where you're going, you'll end up somewhere else."

If you do half of what I suggested in this book, you'll be further down the road to making real changes in your attitudes, your actions and your results.

While this material is fresh in your mind, let's take time to review that list of your insights, your personal *Keepers.* You are going to be moving your passion into practice. Develop a *Bias for Action*; it will get you beyond the head nodding and into an action initiative.

Here's an important tip: don't focus on *more than three Keepers at any one time.* The more goals you give yourself at any given time, the less likely you are to do any of them well. By limiting your focus to only three Keepers or goals, you'll probably see progress where it counts. Make these goals as specific as possible.

Don't worry about making your list perfect. You don't need flawless goals; you just need to trust your ability to concentrate on bringing the ones you have picked to fruition.

Keeping your communication goals top of mind may be easier than you think. *There is no better reminder than your existing calendar system,* because you have to process calendar changes daily. Having your goals visible there in some way makes it much easier to keep your focus on them.

Some people use a small Post-It to move their goals around their paper calendar or to-do-list on a daily basis; others make them visible in computerized to-do lists or online calendars. But wherever you put them, develop the habit of re-reading your three goals each day before you look at your daily schedule.

To maintain unshakable confidence in this journey of self-improvement, don't forget to end your day by recording at least one successful step you took to further your targeted communication goals. When you record—and see—your own progress, you're more likely to create momentum for change.

Here's another important catalyst for personal change: it comes much more easily with a good dose of support from your partners, buddies, bosses, mentors and resident cheerleaders. Choose people who encourage you, who love to celebrate your accomplishments with you. Go beyond telling them about your goals; ask for their help in achieving them. Let them know that you expect change to be difficult, and ask them to alert you if they see your former poor communication habits creep back into your life.

Not everybody will respond to the same strategies to make changes last. However, there is a classic four-step process for turning new concepts, or Keepers, into new habits.

Think about when you first learned how to drive a car. Before you learned how, you were in the "ignorance" stage. You did not know how to drive the car and you did not even know what you didn't know. When you began taking lessons from a driving instructor, you migrated to the second phase: "awareness." You still couldn't drive, but because of your new awareness of the automobile and its parts, you were consciously aware of why you couldn't drive. At this point, the "awareness" stage, you at least realized what you had to do to acquire the competency to drive. You may have felt overwhelmed by the tasks before you, but when these tasks were broken down one by one, they were not so overwhelming after all. They became attainable. Step by step, familiarity replaced fear.

With some additional practice and guidance, you were able to become competent in driving the car through recognition of what you had to do. However, you had to be consciously aware of what you were doing with all of the mechanical aspects of the car as well as with your body. You had to be consciously aware of turning on your blinker signals well before you executed a turn. You had to remember to monitor the traffic behind you in your rearview mirror. You kept both hands on the wheel and noted your car's position relative to the centerline road divider. You were consciously aware of all of these things as you competently drove the car. This third phase is the hardest stage—the one in which you may want to give up. This is the "practice" stage. You'll make mistakes here. This tends to make people uncomfortable, but this is an integral part of the "practice" stage. People experience stress when they implement new behaviors, especially when they perform them imperfectly. Be aware that this stress is very likely to cause you revert to old, more comfortable behaviors, even if those behaviors are less productive.

Your support team can play a crucial role at this point by helping you through the rough spots. They can reinforce the fact that it is alright to make mistakes. In fact, it is necessary to make mistakes, so you can improve through practice, practice and more practice. Your support team can encourage you over these hurdles, and you will reap the harvest of your perseverance.

Let's get back to driving the car and think about the last time that you drove. Were you consciously aware of all of the actions that we just mentioned? Of course not! Most of us, after driving awhile, progress to a level of "habitual performance." This is the level where we can do something well and do not have to think about the steps. They come naturally because they have been so well practiced and they have shifted to automatic pilot. This final stage, then, is when practice results in assimilation and habit.

When you were learning to drive the car, you acquired your competency through practice and perseverance. The same holds true for turning your Keepers from the Great Communicators new habits.

You need to go through the competency processes to get to the highest level, the unconscious competence level. This is where you can communicate naturally and effectively. However, you have to pay a price to get to the level of unconscious competence: Practice, practice, practice.

After persistence and practice, and as you approach the unconscious competency level, your interpersonal communication skills will increase beyond their previous level to a new and higher plateau.

Here's a tip. If you like listening to music on your iPod like I do, take your favorite Keepers or quotes from this program and record them on a digital recorder or on your computer and upload it to your iPod or MP3 player. Now, in the midst of your music, you'll hear some reminders and quotes that will keep you on focus.

I also have an almost endless supply of targeted Dr. Tony Tips on my website at Alessandra.com. The biggest point is to find ways to reinforce daily what you have learned here.

And don't forget to reward and celebrate your own progress. Enjoy the journey you are taking. After all, you don't often *lose* sleep thinking about how great your day was.

I have given you different strategies you can use toward make lasting change more likely. However you use them, resolve to never give up on becoming the great communicator you want to become.

Change rarely comes in the form of instant gratification. If you are like most people, you want success yesterday. Television has exposed most of us to more than a million incredibly unrealistic 30 to 60 second solutions. These ads teach us to expect immediate rewards and results, but life teaches us that real solutions take work, persistence, and time. As many professional coaches and speakers have said, "Motivation is when your dreams put on work clothes." This is not a time to slack off; it is the time to push for the summit on the horizon.

If your changes are worth making, it is worth persevering to find a way to achieve them. Norman Vincent Peale had a plaque on his wall that read: "Anybody Can Quit!"

Coach Bear Bryant would remind his players: "Don't give up at half-time. Concentrate on winning the second half."

Be patient but persistent. You do not know which day and which step will put your goals within reach. When it seems like you are not making progress, keep your perspective. Your next step for change may produce the breakthrough you are seeking.

Part of being persistent is doing something positive every day. Life is best taken one day at a time, no matter what changes we seek. The most important changes have to be earned again and again every single day. Don't waste any of them. Be flexible, realistic, and practical. Focus on your mission, your goals, your best, your choices, and your progress. Use every day, because every day matters.

If you have decided to accept the challenge of more effectively communicating with others, the payoffs are certainly well worth your efforts. With so much to learn about, you might be confused as to where to start. My advice is that you first assess your current situation. How well do you do you probe? Or listen? Or read body language? How about give and receive feedback? Do you communicate effectively with time and space?

Determine your current situation and compare it with your new objectives and then identify those areas that need work. There may be a number of areas that need work, but take care to set priorities on problem areas according to how much attention they need. Develop an action plan to improve those areas. Define what has to be done to accomplish your action plan. Set up an implementation schedule, and establish commitment to follow it through according to the scheduled completion times. Set goals and establish your criteria for success; determine how and when to measure your performance in improving your interpersonal communication skills. Then, constantly monitor the results, and take corrective action where necessary.

Your new action plan might include further professional help in the form of seminars, books, or tapes. Keep informed of other learning devices that will help you improve any or all of the skills discussed in this program. Your plan may also include a more detailed review of relevant portions of this book when appropriate.

You can start to apply communication skills immediately. The path has been mapped. Where you go from here depends on your determination and persistence in applying these skills.

We've covered a lot of ground in this book and studied a number of truly remarkable communication skills. Before we conclude, I think it would be helpful to mention some of the skills that didn't make my top ten list but are significant and warrant your attention after you begin to master the top ten. These include the importance of having confidence, which will grow as you master the top ten. Infusing a sense of humor into your communications can be engaging and even disarming when used appropriately. It is important to develop the compelling attitude of gratitude, which others will sense, making them more receptive to your message. Storytelling is another skill that can be a powerful vehicle for delivering your message or making a point. One final skill is understanding your audience. Knowing what is important to the person or group you're addressing or interacting with will help you prepare and deliver your message so it will be most effective.

I would like to say you have everything you need to perform as a great communicator with these qualities and skills. But there is one thing all great communicators have in common that I have not mentioned yet and it is of critical importance. Find role models and mentors who are great communicators.

These are people to admire and emulate, and it is worthwhile to analyze the constructive characteristics of great communicators who are where you would like to be. Your choices can include people who are living or dead as long as you are familiar with their personalities and accomplishments.

Harry Truman knew the value of role models. When he was in the White House he often went into the Lincoln bedroom, looked at the late president's picture and asked, "What would Lincoln have done now?" The answers gave Truman the insight and direction he was seeking. It worked because Truman felt Lincoln was a man worth emulating.

How do you go about choosing a role model that can inspire you? The following guidelines can really help:

- Keep them off a pedestal. It's good to admire and emulate them because of what they have accomplished. What is not good is putting them above you and trying to make them appear larger than life. We are all human. We all have strengths and weaknesses. You must not lose this perspective.

- Focus on the strong points of the great communicators. See what behaviors you might need to emulate and make a conscious effort to model those qualities. It is a responsibility on the part of great communicators, not unlike being a parent, but one so many have willingly taken on. Edison had a whole army of assistants and colleagues who viewed him as a role model, as did Walt Disney. Many of them went on to do great things in their own right.

- Above all, remain yourself. The tendency when admiring a role model can be to become his or her clone. A great communicator does not encourage that. A great communicator wants to be around other great communicators, not wannabes. That is why the ability to bring out the communication genius in others is so rewarding.

So—go for it! Put all of this into action, and let it take you where you are destined to go. Make the journey your intention, not the outcome.

CPSIA information can be obtained
at www.ICGtesting.com
Printed in the USA
JSHW031356061120
9390JS00001B/11

9 781722 500269